HOW TO
A CASTLE
AND HOW TO DEFEND IT

Trevor Yorke

COUNTRYSIDE BOOKS
NEWBURY BERKSHIRE

COUNTRYSIDE BOOKS
3 Catherine Road
Newbury, Berkshire

To view our complete range of books,
please visit us at
www.countrysidebooks.co.uk

ISBN 978 1 84674 366 5

Illustrations and modern photographs by Trevor Yorke

Designed and Typeset by KT Designs, St Helens
Produced through The Letterworks Ltd., Reading
Printed by The Holywell Press, Oxford

Contents

Introduction

Mighty battlements exploding as projectiles flung from huge timber catapults send masonry flying. Balls of fire leaving arced trails of smoke through the air until they crash into buildings, setting them alight. Colossal tree trunks hung under wheeled shelters with iron caps shaped like a beast smashing through the towering wooden gates. Brave armour-clad knights valiantly fighting back the enemy to prevent them from taking their castle. These exciting images of battles between the attackers and defenders of the mighty stone fortifications are familiar to us from books, films and television. From Tolkien to *Game of Thrones* they have helped fire a passion for a fantasy medieval world. However the reality of warfare in the period could be very different and the way in which castles were forced into submission or resisted an enemy were more varied and interesting than just a show of brute force.

In this book I set out to introduce you to the real medieval castle and the machines, weapons and tactics used by both attackers and defenders. It will outline the nature of siege warfare in Britain during different periods, taking you on a journey through time from the earliest motte and bailey castles erected by the conquering Normans to those built by Edward I to try to suppress the Welsh. Along the way I will show you the new methods and inventions used by attackers to try and break through walls or frighten those inside the castle into surrender, at the same time explaining how the defenders adapted the fortifications to counter any new threat. There will also be short accounts of real-life sieges, from the dramatic to the humorous, which help to illustrate how human factors played a large part in the success or not of an attack.

The book uses many of my own photographs, illustrations and diagrams, not only to explain the reality of siege warfare but also to enhance your visits to the many wonderful castles which still exist in our country. Some remain almost complete, often turned into magnificent museums; some have been shorn of their defences – mostly by Oliver Cromwell after the Civil War; others are in ruins with only a wall to show where they once stood. But all of them have a story to tell, and after reading this book I hope you will be able to recognise parts of each of them through the crumbling walls and grassy mounds that conceal defensive features, built when military necessity or ambition and power dictated it.

Whether you are young or old the world of castles is full of excitement, wonder and surprise, with hundreds

of mighty buildings just waiting to be explored.

Trevor Yorke

Follow me on Facebook at
trevoryorke-author
Or visit my website:
www.trevoryorke.co.uk

FIG 0.1: A castle under siege with labels highlighting some of the key features.

 # MEDIEVAL SIEGE WARFARE
Kings, Knights and Castles

In the medieval world kingdoms were won, monarchs toppled and nobles gained new lands through the successful attack upon, or defence of, a castle. Those who tried to capture the fortification could launch a surprise attack or besiege it for weeks and sometimes even months, often resorting to extraordinary actions in order to break through the defences. They used siege engines to pound the walls, archers to pick men off the tops of the walls, and sent incendiary devices over the battlements to set fire to the buildings within. Tunnels were dug under the walls; sappers sent up to pick at the masonry in order to create a breach; siege towers and ladders were used for an assault over the top. Some attackers even fired contaminated corpses into the castle to spread disease, or they had prisoners executed in front of horrified defenders to try and induce surrender.

Medieval commanders were not afraid to employ deception and intrigue with devious tricks used to try and enter the castle gates or have spies planted inside to find out vital information. If a direct attack failed then the defenders, cut off from gaining fresh supplies, could eventually have to surrender through starvation or lack of water. Medieval siege warfare was not a rapid process and much of a medieval king's, baron's and knight's time and money was spent attacking an enemy's castles or defending their own.

Those trapped within did not just sit down and wait for the inevitable end. Sieges were two-way battles and the defenders were just as likely to go onto the offensive. They too had siege engines which could take out enemy weapons and personnel. They had giant crossbows which could pierce armour and shields and they used fire to destroy the attackers' machinery. Most castles had a discreet rear exit so soldiers could slip out at night and raid the enemy camp, take hostages, or get a message out to send for a relieving force. Defenders upon the battlements had the advantage of height so heavy objects and red hot substances could be dropped around the walls or gates while archers had a good line of sight to shoot unwary attackers below. King Richard I, idealised as one of our great monarchs

FIG 1.1: The moment in late November 1215 when, after nearly two months of besieging Rochester Castle, Kent, military miners working for King John finally brought down the corner of the mighty stone keep. This unpopular monarch had broken his promises made in the Magna Carta, so rebel barons rose up against him, capturing a number of key castles including Rochester. The king's forces had attacked the defences with crossbows and missiles, and bombarded its walls with siege engines. But, it was only when they undermined its fortifications by digging tunnels beneath the structure that they finally broke through. Despite this, the defenders held on within one half of the keep for a further few days before surrendering when their supplies ran out.

despite spending only a few months of his ten-year reign in this country, was inspecting progress on the siege of a small French castle when he was shot by a crossbow bolt fired from the battlements by a boy and he died a few weeks later from the wound. So although attackers would seem to have the upper hand with their wide range of weapons and tactics, in most cases defenders still had a few countermeasures available, and in some cases they could even turn the situation to their advantage. From the Norman invasion in 1066 through to the early 14th century castles were the centre point of military activity in Britain and through them the fate of a king, prince or noble could be decided.

Why were castles so important?

Why did medieval commanders go to great lengths to capture or disable castles? Part of the reason was that

FIG 1.2: The castle was built upon a high point with a towering form not just to be impenetrable but also to overawe the conquered population. Its formidable defences, battlements and huge towers sent a message to them that the owner and his troops were an immovable and invincible force which was there for the long term. King Edward I had this in mind when he built Caernarfon Castle, pictured here, which became the centre of English rule over the Principality of Wales after his victorious campaign in the 1280s.

most medieval kings were wary about major battles, which they saw as unpredictable and dangerous events in which an army could be wiped out in a matter of hours. A war could be fought with the forces split across a number of sieges so that if one failed all was not lost. Many early castles were positioned to guard a key route or a river crossing so an invading army would have to pass by thus making them vulnerable to attack. Some castle ruins can be found today at the head of a lonely valley or by a seemingly minor bridge because when they were founded these were either important routes or the only crossing in the area. If an army tried to bypass these strategically placed fortifications then it could add days onto a march, which would give the enemy time to prepare. It could also cause problems because the garrison in the castle could ride out and disrupt their supply chain. In 1216, when Prince Louis of France invaded Southern England and marched into London, he neglected to first disable the castles which stood between his army and the south coast where his supplies were landed. As a result, the garrison at Dover Castle constantly disrupted his supply chain taking up so much time and resources that his invasion faltered and he was ultimately paid off to refute his claim to be King of England. Castles were also important because they were not just a military establishment but also the home of a king or noble. Unlike earlier Roman forts which were purely military bases, or Saxon burhs which were fortified towns, castles were designed to accommodate both an armed garrison and the wealthy owner and his household. Anyone trying to take over a territory could not claim to be the new incumbent

Who lived in the castle?

The castle was the home of a king, lord or knight, although sometimes a lady might be in control when her husband was absent or had died. Monarchs had their own royal castles which they would constantly travel between. Their number fluctuated as some were granted to feudal vassals as a reward while others were confiscated in punishment. The majority of castles however were in the hands of lords and knights who were responsible for keeping order over their fiefdom or manor and providing military service when called upon. In the absence of the owner, castles were run by the castellan, castelain or constable, a role which could include responsibility for the garrison of soldiers as well as the daily running of the fortification. As a king and his nobles would have a number of castles and could only be at one place at any time it was often the castelain who defended the building and organised the garrison when it was besieged. The castle was a busy place even in times of peace with soldiers training, blacksmiths making and repairing weapons and armour, and carpenters and masons building. The outer bailey or ward not only contained workshops and storage for supplies but also the men's accommodation and stables for the horses.

until the previous one had been removed from his castle.

How to conduct a siege

As the fate of a kingdom could centre upon gaining control of castles, the attack and defence of them had to be thoroughly planned. The first approach in most situations was to try and avoid a siege by allowing the garrison to surrender. This was regarded as a chivalric move (the chivalric code was an unwritten code of chivalrous social behavior between knights and nobles) in part to protect the unnecessary loss of nobles and knights, but it also made sense because a siege would be an expensive process for both sides and could result in damage to the castle which would then be costly for the victor to repair. Sometimes the reputation of a feared commander or a huge army might force the garrison to throw open the gates of a castle before they had even arrived. In other cases, diplomacy or bribery could be used so that a compromise was reached by which the castle would be spared as long as it did not then threaten the attacker's progress.

As a monarch or lord usually had a number of castles each one was left in the hands of his castelain or garrison commander. If they were unclear on their instructions or were unable to communicate with their master, they might be more susceptible to

FIG 1.3: Castles were generally located in a strategic military position or in a location where they could control the local population and trade. They were very rarely positioned on top of the highest hill but were sited lower down in a dominant position close to river crossings, the head of a valley or in a town or city. Many were located on a natural promontory or mound while others were built on relatively flat land so that artificial mottes, ditches and moats had to be created as defensive measures. It was also common for a new town to be established or to develop close to the castle as here at Dunster Castle, Somerset. Although this would seem to be an advantage for the inhabitants as they could seek refuge if an army approached, they were often kicked out of the castle if supplies got low and could be massacred by attackers frustrated that they could not break though the walls.

surrender. In other cases, if the owner of the castles had been captured then he could be forced to send orders for them to open the gates.

If a fight was inevitable then both sides usually had a little time to prepare. Some commanders had access to the works of the Roman military author Vegetius and were influenced by his belief in extensive training, thorough preparation, and waiting to make a decisive move when victory was virtually guaranteed. Those defending the castle would have to make sure they had good supplies of food and a reliable source of water, as well as the materials to enhance their defences and a stock of weapons plus the carpenters and blacksmiths to make and repair them. Those besieging would need the same and as the area around the castle might have been burned or cleared of such supplies before their arrival they might have to wait some time before they could commence their attack. Timing was also an issue for a military planner. Late spring and early summer was the best time to attack when the weather was favourable. The stock of food in the castle would be low and water was liable to run out. For a besieger, winter was usually avoided due to the wet and cold while many of those serving would frequently go back to their homes in order to sow seeds early in the year. The same difficulty applied at harvest time towards the end of the year. The commander of the garrison was penned into his castle, but even he had to consider the soldiers and knights who were serving as part of their feudal duties. This commitment to help with the defence, known as castle guard, only lasted for a set period, typically around two to three months a year, so they were within their rights to walk

The Roman Influence

Many medieval kings often saw themselves as natural successors to the Romans. Medieval clerics translated surviving texts from the ancient Roman authors such as Vitruvius and Vegetius, which would have given them access to some of the empire's military tactics and the design of both their defensive structures and siege engines. As the Roman Empire had survived around Constantinople, medieval kings and knights may also have been influenced by the forts and weapons they came across while on the crusades. In addition, there were the remains which the Romans had left behind in this country. They had built mighty stone and brick walls for their forts and town defences; most spectacularly along much of Hadrian's Wall. They had towers and gatehouses which were designed to resist an attack and above all, a network of well-built roads which could give their forces a direct route so they could respond quickly to any incident. Many of the earliest castles were established on the site of a Roman fort or were built reusing the material from their defensive walls.

FIG 1.4: Castles were multifunctional centres for a town or territory. They were a military base from which armed knights and soldiers could venture out and suppress rebellion or raid neighbouring land. Castles were the home of a king or noble so could have a grand hall and fine accommodation. There would also be room for the numerous household servants and carts full of belongings that the owner travelled with between visits to their properties. They would usually only stay a matter of weeks at each one.

The high walls and towers were essential as look-out posts to warn of approaching armies and the rooms underground were vital to store supplies in case of a siege or the arrival of the owner. Castles also became the administrative centre of a territory, from where a lord could carry out his feudal role, soldiers could patrol the area, courts could be held and prisoners thrown in jail. Many castles have survived into the modern age because they were convenient courtrooms and prisons long after their military value had faded. Norwich Castle, pictured here, still has the old prison buildings which were added to the rear of this mighty Norman keep.

out if a siege extended beyond this time. As this could be inconvenient for both parties it became common for them to give their lord a payment rather than serve, money which could be spent on better trained and dedicated mercenaries who would be expected to fight to the end.

Once the castle had been surrounded the attackers would often go on the rampage, raiding the surrounding towns and villages for loot and burning the countryside to deprive the castle of supplies if this had not already been done by the defenders. Initially men would have been kept occupied erecting siege engines, digging ditches, raising banks and in some cases building temporary castles so the besiegers would be safe from a surprise attack. If a siege dragged on then keeping the morale up of those inside and outside the castle could soon become a problem. The constant pounding of stone balls smashing into walls or the dead bodies of colleagues being catapulted into the castle could take their toll on the mental state of those trapped inside. The attackers could equally become demoralised if they saw that their attempts to break through were constantly failing. A deal which was sometimes struck allowed the castelain or commander to send out a message to his master for instruction on whether to continue the defence of the castle on the promise that if he did not receive a reply within an agreed time he would surrender. Sometimes a belligerent commander might persist with a siege despite the castle being impenetrable or the defenders might refuse all offers in the belief that they might be saved by a relieving force before they ran out of supplies. It could often take an act of treachery or a clever deception to finally bring matters to a head. Most likely though, when a siege dragged on into months, it was disease or starvation which finally resulted in the gates being swung open. Whoever was the first to break would want an honourable end to proceedings so they could hold their heads high rather than be slaughtered in a fight to the death. The successful attacker might take his frustration and vengeance out on a few defenders and the poor townsfolk, but usually the knights and nobles were allowed to walk out unharmed.

MOTTE AND BAILEY CASTLES
Timber, Fire and Arrows

When, in 1066, William, Duke of Normandy, sought to establish his right to the English throne, his first action after he crossed the channel was to build a castle within the old Roman fortification at Pevensey, Sussex. After the victory a short way along the south coast at Hastings, William was faced with the problem of having to control his new territory with an army and entourage which probably numbered around 20,000 in a country of 1,500,000 potentially rebellious Saxons. In order for such a limited number of Normans to hold key strategic points and also strike fear so that the native population would be reluctant to rise up against them, William had to quickly establish a network of castles.

William was of Viking descent and the title Norman is derived from Norseman. He had even brought some flat-packed fortified structures across the channel with him to speed up their construction. Many were built by his victorious barons on land William granted them in return for their loyalty. The first were erected along the coast to protect the landing points for his supplies and then as he pushed inland more were built to control valleys and river crossings. Some were also established in urban areas and many of these were purposely sited within existing fortifications, old Roman forts and Saxon burhs. He was not only saving time by reusing part of their defensive structures but also depriving the native population of a point from which to rebel. With these new imposing castles stamped upon Saxon towns and cities William was making it clear that he was in control and they would have to submit to his authority.

The new castles which were established across the country by William and his barons were usually of a motte and bailey design. This new type of fortification had evolved in Western Europe over the preceding century as kingdoms broke up into smaller units governed by nobles who needed a defendable home during these turbulent times. The bailey was a large enclosed area for the garrison, horses and supplies surrounded by a timber wall or palisade. It was overlooked by the motte, a tall mound upon which

14

FIG 2.1: Attackers fighting their way through the bailey while fire arrows rain down upon the tower on top of the motte. Defenders have draped fresh raw hides over the timber wall to reduce the chances of it catching fire.

FIG 2.2: York Castle: William faced numerous rebellions during the first few years of his reign, the most troublesome area being the north of England. Here he installed Robert de Comines as his Earl of Northumbria only for his army of 700 men to be slaughtered by a rebel force on the streets of Durham and the Earl burnt to death when they set fire to his home. The rebels then marched south and took the castle at York but were killed or scattered when William arrived to relieve it. Later in 1069 they tried again and retook the city and besieged the castle. As the Norman defenders sneaked out of the fortification to burn parts of the city which could be used by the attackers they were overrun and the castle was taken. When William returned again to face the rebels they melted away but this time the king lost his patience and set out to destroy the surrounding region which had supported them, by raiding and burning villages and towns in an act known as the Harrying of the North. The motte of York Castle is pictured here with the stone shell keep around its top added at a later date.

stood a timber lookout tower and refuge, known as the keep or donjon, which also provided accommodation for the noble or owner. The two were connected by gated bridge or steps which may have been removable in part at a time of trouble. The motte and bailey castle was a flexible form which could be adapted to the different sites. There were however, some occasions where a simpler form of earthwork was used. Ringwork castles, an enclosure formed from a defensive ditch, bank and palisades with the buildings erected within were often used, especially where there were existing fortifications or where a stone keep was planned which needed to be built upon a secure flat area.

These imposing fortifications made from wood and earth had the advantage that they could be built quickly as most men had the required building skills and the materials were readily available. The soil dug out when forming the ditches that surrounded the castle could be used to build up the bailey and the motte (the word motte was Norman for hillock). Timber for the structures could be sourced from the local area as well as from the houses and other buildings, which were often ruthlessly cleared off the site to make way for the castle. Although most buildings and walls were built from wood until the second half of the following century, in parts of the north and west stone was readily available and could have been used at an early date for some structures.

Attacking a Motte and Bailey Castle

The motte and bailey castle was a formidable obstacle for any army. The motte was designed with steep sides so it could not be scaled by men on horseback, and would be difficult for those on foot too. Some may have been covered in clay or timber to help protect the mound's structure and make a surface which was harder to get a foothold upon. Thorn bushes could have also been planted to form a further barrier. It was the bailey which made the easier target for an attacking force and would be the first point where they would concentrate their efforts. Men with axes could hack at the timber palisades while shields or protective covers held off the defender's arrows. In many cases the castle was simply stormed by a superior force who overwhelmed the defenders, attacking them with volleys of arrows, scaling the walls on ladders, and making their way through the castle with hand-to-hand fighting. When William II attacked rebels at Tonbridge Castle in 1088 he did not wait for machines to be built, but charged straight into direct action, taking the fortification within two days.

There was one weapon however which became the first choice for forces attacking a timber castle, and that was fire. Archers could shoot flaming arrows directly at the walls or aim higher and let them rain down upon the buildings behind them. Some arrowheads were designed with small oval-shaped metal cages behind the point specifically to contain natural fibres or cloth soaked in pitch for this purpose. William II's brother, Robert of Normandy, ordered his bowmen to heat up the metal tips of their arrows in a fire until red hot and then shoot them onto the castle buildings. The defenders did not realise these arrows were setting fire to the roof until it was too late. The Bayeux Tapestry shows men setting fire to the timber palisades with firebrands on long poles so presumably this was a tried and tested method. There are also records of early attempts of making incendiary devices. A clay vessel filled with a mixture containing an inflammable substance like pitch, tar or animal fat was ignited and thrown at the walls, smashing on impact and forming a fire which would be hard for defenders to extinguish. These could have been dispatched by hand, thrown using a staff sling (a pole with a sling at the end) or by catapult. Geoffrey Plantagenet, the Count of Anjou and father of Henry II, became something of an expert in the use of fire and made an

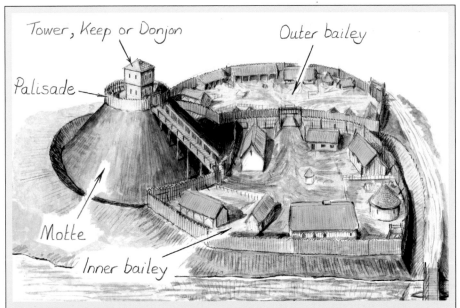

Tower, Keep or Donjon

Outer bailey

Palisade

Motte

Inner bailey

FIG 2.3: A view showing how the motte and bailey castle in Tonbridge, Kent, may have looked after it was erected by Richard Fitz Gilbert in the aftermath of the victory at Hastings. Mottes were not just a huge lump of earth but a carefully constructed structure and were usually built up in layers or around a rubble core where there was not an existing natural mound that could be used. They could vary from 50ft to over 100ft high and could have a diameter up to 300ft across. A timber palisade, a tall defensive wall made of vertical planks or logs, would have been erected around the keep or donjon on top. There is uncertainty as to the exact design of these buildings as evidence is sparse, mainly coming from stylised images on the Bayeux tapestry or descriptions from contemporary writers. It is likely they were simple timber structures in order to keep the weight down on the earthen motte and so they could be erected quickly by soldiers and local labour. Richard Fitz Gilbert's original motte and bailey castle had a short life, as when the Conqueror died in 1087 he sided with his eldest son Robert, rather than the younger William. The latter however took the throne of England and besieged Richard's castle at Tonbridge. After only two days, he stormed the defences and burnt it to the ground. The motte still survives today within the remains of the later stone castle.

iron cauldron containing flax, seed and oil, which was heated up and thrown at the gates of the castle he was besieging so that it exploded on contact and set them on fire.

Defending a Motte and Bailey Castle

The defence of many castles began before an attacking army was in sight.

The area around the outer walls could be cleared; this required demolishing houses and burning fields. The local drinking water could be poisoned and all good timber collected and stored inside the castle so the enemy could not use it. When the defenders of Wolvesey Castle, Winchester were preparing for an attack from the Empress Matilda in 1141, they burnt all the houses close to the walls which could give the enemy cover. In doing so they accidentally destroyed a large part of the old city. Carpenters and blacksmiths could also be forced inside the castle to help with making arms and also to ensure they were not available to assist the enemy.

With fire being the greatest threat, defenders could try and soak the timbers or drape fresh or wet animal

The Chaos of Stephen and Matilda's Reign

The successful Norman conquest of England and parts of Wales had only been possible because of the firm grip that William the Conqueror and his sons William II and Henry I were able to exert upon their powerful barons and the native population. This extended to the construction of castles which had to be authorised by the King so he could ensure none of his subjects would have their fortifications consolidated in one area and have a powerful base which could threaten the crown. However, when Henry's only son died in 1120 a succession crisis loomed.

The king made preparations so that he would be succeeded by his daughter, Matilda, who in 1128 married Geoffrey Plantagenet, the Count of Anjou. However, many barons were not so keen on this idea and some supported the claim of Stephen of Blois, the son of one of William the Conqueror's daughters. When Henry died in 1135 it was Stephen who moved first and seized the throne. Trouble soon broke out and some barons rose up in rebellion. King David of Scotland invaded from the north and Geoffrey fought for control of Normandy. If that was not enough, in 1139 Matilda invaded England. This civil war was to last for the following 14 years, with fortunes swinging this way then that. Stephen was captured by Matilda in 1141 and she was almost crowned queen but was then forced to release him and only just escaped with her own life when she had to sneak out of the besieged Oxford Castle on a frozen winter's night. Matters came to a head in 1153 when Matilda's eldest son, Henry, faced off the King's forces at Wallingford Castle, Oxon.

However, with both sides weary of the conflict an agreement was struck so that Stephen would make Matilda's son his successor when he died, an act which brought the war to an end. This civil war, referred to as The Anarchy by Victorian historians, was mainly played out around the sieges of castles. With the breakdown of royal power during this period numerous illegal motte and bailey castles were erected as nobles sought to grab land off their enemies while the king was occupied with his disputed crown. A large number of the motte and bailey castles which survive as grassy mounds and ditches around the country today were at their peak in this turbulent period and declined in use and influence once it ended.

FIG 2.4: Warwick Castle: This mighty medieval fortification and palatial home to the Earls of Warwick was originally a humbler motte and bailey castle established by William the Conqueror. The second Earl, Roger de Beaufort, seems to have played both sides during The Anarchy, originally supporting Empress Matilda but then fighting with King Stephen in 1153 while he left his castle at Warwick under the stewardship of his wife with a garrison of royal troops. However, Matilda's son, Henry, and his knights tricked her into believing that the Earl was dead and she ejected the garrison and handed the castle over to Henry's men. Legend has it that upon hearing the news that his castle had been lost the Earl suddenly died due to his shame and grief.

hides over the palisades. The walls may have been coated in limewash or perhaps daub (a rendering made from clay, straw and other ingredients) in an attempt to make the timber more fire resistant. Water, sand, ash and earth may have been used by defenders to throw over any parts of the fortifications which had caught fire. If the enemy broke into the bailey then the garrison could retreat to the motte and destroy any bridge between the two, making an effective last stand. As the motte was on the outer edge of the bailey it also gave the defenders the chance to escape down the slope if all was lost. However, there was also the

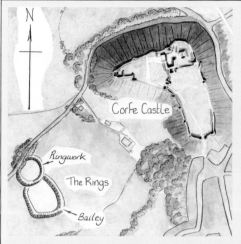

FIG 2.5: Siege castles: If the attack upon a castle was going to be a long, drawn-out affair then some attackers built a fortification referred to as a siege castle. The remains of one example can still be seen to the south west of Corfe Castle, Dorset (as shown on this map), and is assumed to have been formed when King Stephen unsuccessfully besieged this mighty stone castle in 1139. Siege castles may have been no more than an enclosure surrounded by ditches and banks, more of a temporary fort than a fully-fledged castle. As in the example at Corfe they were carefully positioned just out of range of the defenders' weapons and gave protection to attackers from an assault at the rear from relieving forces and allowed them to make sure no one could leave the besieged castle. They were often built when the attacking commander decided to move onto another project and wanted to leave a small force behind to hold the besieged castle. In 1095 the Earl of Northumberland, Robert de Mowbray, after having conspired against King William II, barricaded himself in his castle at Bamburgh as the king's forces approached. This formidable fortress was clearly going to take time to defeat so William II erected a temporary siege castle nearby which he referred to as a Malvoisin – an evil neighbour. However, Mowbray was able to escape, only to be captured later and forced to hand over Bamburgh Castle when the king threatened to blind him.

FIG 2.6: Oxford Castle: During The Anarchy, Matilda made Oxford her campaign base. In response King Stephen moved in to besiege this formidable castle and capture her. His troops, on the opposite side of the Thames, were taunted by the defenders so Stephen and some of his men swam across the river and stormed the city before surrounding the fortification and setting up siege castles to make sure no one could escape. Matilda's supporters tried to draw Stephen away but with no effect. Legend has it that one snowy winter's night, after the siege had dragged on for months, Matilda, dressed in white, slipped out of the castle and managed to pass through the attackers without them noticing her. Once she was safely away the castle garrison surrendered to the disappointed Stephen. St George's Tower (pictured) was built in 1074 and would have been standing at the time of the siege.

FIG 2.7: Since ancient times, fire was used by attackers to destroy fortifications which contained timber structures. Lit torches or fires set up against a wooden wall were probably the earliest type of incendiary device. Flaming arrows were used in the medieval period as, even after castle walls were built of masonry, there was still wood in the roofs and floors of stone buildings and lesser timber structures within the enclosure. The arrow could have been crudely assembled with a strip of material soaked in pitch, oil or resin wrapped around the shaft. More sophisticated arrowheads were designed with metal cages for coal, wood shavings, cloth or similar materials soaked in oil, which were then lit and fired. A more potent weapon which struck fear into the hearts of defenders was 'Greek fire', a petroleum-based mixture which could not be extinguished with water. The knowledge for making this mixture (an early form of napalm) came via the Crusades to the Middle East in the 11th century where siege warfare was far more advanced than it was in Western Europe. Although the exact contents varied and its use was probably limited in this country, there are records of experts being paid to make Greek fire for attack on later stone castles. Richard I used some form of Greek fire when he was besieging Nottingham Castle in 1194 and pots were ordered to contain an explosive mixture during the siege of Stirling Castle in 1304. In 1340 at Tournai, France, Edward III's forces employed a man who successfully created Greek fire to use against the defenders only for him to vanish without a trace after he had received payment in advance for more of his secret concoction.

terrifying possibility that they could be trapped within a burning ring of fire, with any defenders trying to douse the flames picked off by archers.

Once the dispute was over, the crown had been settled and the new king Henry II had a firm grip over his kingdom, there began a great shift in the design of castles. Timber motte and bailey castles which had been erected without royal approval were demolished. Those which by the 1150s no longer served a military role were abandoned. Many fortifications which remained, especially those in the hands of the Crown or his wealthiest nobles, were extended and rebuilt. The revised fortifications had to adapt not only to the threat of fire as the knowledge of how to make and use it became more widespread, but also to the threat of new siege engines which could throw stones and smash timber palisades. Hence from the mid-12th century, castles were increasingly rebuilt in stone.

FIG 2.8: Motte of Urr, Dumfries and Galloway: After up to 900 years of weathering many mottes and baileys have shrunken to a fraction of their original form. Some however remain remarkably intact and imposing as here at the Motte of Urr, Scotland. This castle was built in around 1165 by Walter de Berkeley, a Norman settler in this region, which had remained relatively independent of the Kings of Scotland. However, when locals rose up in rebellion against their Lord in 1174 they first blinded, castrated and murdered him, then set about attacking Norman property, including Urr, burning it to the ground. It was rebuilt with a taller motte, but after the turn of the 14th century it seems to have been abandoned.

THE GREAT STONE KEEPS
Battlements, Mining and Mangonels

The castle in the late 12th and early 13th century

As Henry II imposed his grip upon the throne after the death of King Stephen in 1154 he set about demolishing or rendering indefensible (slighting) numerous castles which had been erected without royal consent or which could threaten his position. Despite his effective rule, Henry had to face numerous threats to his throne. Barons were still keen to revolt and even his own sons rebelled against the king for a while. When Henry died in 1189, Richard I became king but despite his historic reputation as good King Richard, the Lionheart, he probably spent only a few months of his ten-year reign in the country and was killed while besieging a castle in France. Henry's youngest son John, followed Richard on the throne, was less successful as a monarch and, after managing to lose Normandy and failing to win it back from the French King, he faced a rebellion from his barons unhappy with his rule. In 1215 a peace agreement in which a list of demands and reforms were made of the King, later called

the Great Charter or Magna Carta, did little to quell tensions and armed conflict soon followed. The First Baron's War started well for John as he took Rochester Castle from the barons and in early 1216 pushed King Alexander II of Scotland, who had joined the rebels, back to Edinburgh. The rebel barons turned to the French Prince Louis who was married to the granddaughter of Henry II and hence had a claim to the throne. He invaded with an army later that year but after John died unexpectedly in October his cause petered out as the barons turned their support to the young King Henry III.

Timber motte and bailey castles had served their purpose for the first century of Norman rule but their shortcomings were now becoming evident. Tactics had been developed by attackers to overpower them whilst those returning from crusades brought with them new ideas and weapons from the Middle East. Not only was fire a constant threat but now more powerful siege engines could potentially smash its palisades. In response, those castles

FIG 3.1: Dover Castle was one of the mightiest of medieval fortresses with its huge stone keep and walls high above the chalk cliffs. When Prince Louis of France invaded England in May 1216 at the invitation of barons who were rebelling against King John, he realised too late that he had made a mistake in not first taking this key castle. His delay had given the constable Hubert de Burgh time to prepare and when Louis did finally besiege it in July Dover Castle was able to successfully hold out for three months despite the French prince's best efforts as shown in this image. Even when they were able to bring down part of the walls Hubert de Burgh had already built up a barricade inside so they could not get past. Louis called a truce in October 1216 but the unexpected death of King John that month took away the barons' main reason for rebelling and many turned their support to the new young King Henry III. Prince Louis tried again to break into Dover Castle the following year but this took up so much of his force that his remaining supporters were defeated at Lincoln.

which survived Henry II's culling were increasingly rebuilt in stone. Masonry had been used since the Norman conquest but it was usually reserved for key parts of select royal castles or in areas where stone was plentiful and timber scarce. Its use had been rare up to the mid-12th century as timber castles could be erected and made defendable in a matter of weeks. Skilled masons were expensive and most of them were usually working exclusively for the Crown or the Church. Masonry was also very expensive as quarrying and transport could mean importing the material from miles away and would usually require access to a navigable river as roads were so poor. Caen stone from Normandy was shipped over for projects including the keeps at the Tower of London and Norwich Castle with the stone brought up to site along the adjacent rivers. At Carlisle the troublesome border with Scotland forced Henry I to order the rebuilding of the castle in stone in 1122, a major project which included the construction of defensive walls around the whole city. It was usually these royal castles and those in the hands of the wealthiest nobles, which were built in stone first and then it may have only been part of the castle with timber walls and structures remaining alongside stone ones for many decades.

FIG 3.2: Colchester Castle: One of the first stone keeps built in Britain was erected by William the Conqueror in Colchester. As with many of his early castles it was on the site of a Roman Fort, which not only provided existing earthworks and a source of building materials but also sent out a message that the Normans were emulating the power and authority of Rome. The first storey was probably started in the 1070s with the upper section added in the early 12th century. Despite mostly using existing brick and stone from the site the Norman builders still had to bring over Caen stone for some of the carved details like the doorways.

Stone keeps

The fashion in the 12th century was to retain a single stronghold within the defences. This was usually a keep or donjon placed on firm ground within the old bailey or built on the site of the original motte which was either reduced in height or removed completely. These new stone structures were built on a grander scale than the old timber towers so they could provide a higher standard of accommodation for the owner and

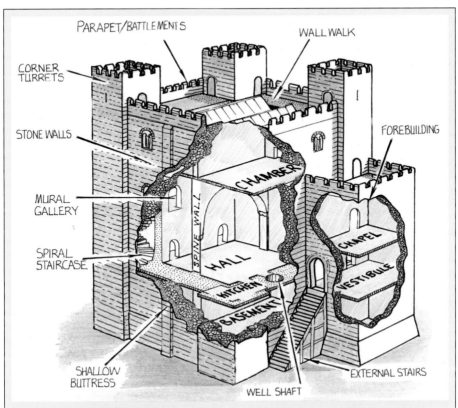

FIG 3.3: The Keep: A cut away drawing of a typical 12th-century stone keep showing a possible arrangement of rooms inside. Most which were built in this period had distinctive shallow buttresses up the walls with thin carved columns set into the outer corners. The stairs were often exposed at first but were later enclosed within a passageway or the forebuilding to give retreating soldiers protection.

improved security at a time of crisis. In some cases, they were positioned above the old gateway so the new structure would help strengthen this defensive weak point. The stone walls were generally very thick so they could withstand the impact of projectiles hurled by siege engines, in some cases around 4-5m (12-15ft) in depth. Most were composed of a facing inside and out of squared blocks of masonry with a thick core of rubble set in mortar, an arrangement which can be seen today in ruined castles. Many may have also had a protective coat of limewash so would have had an off white appearance. In most keeps there would have been a central dividing wall called a spine wall which was important not only to

FIG 3.4: Battlements: It was during this period of stone castle building that the familiar battlements around the top of the keep and defensive walls took shape. They consisted of lengths of vertical parapet called merlons with gaps between known as crenels, hence these toothed features are also known as crenellations. Behind them was the wall walk upon which defenders could act as look outs to warn of an approaching army and take refuge while attacking the besiegers. As an additional protection wooden shutters could be fitted into the crenels with a hinge at the top so archers could push them out to aim and fire and they would then fall shut as they withdrew.

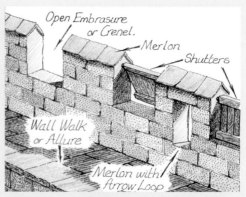

FIG 3.5: Lincoln Castle: This important castle, established by William the Conqueror on the site of a Roman fort, was besieged by forces loyal to Prince Louis in 1217. When they heard that Henry III's army under the command of the formidable William Marshall was approaching they considered open battle outside the city, which if his forces were small would have resulted in certain victory. However, as they were unsure of its size they retreated behind the city gates and continued their siege only for Marshall's forces to storm the city and rain crossbow bolts down upon the panicking besiegers forcing them to flee.

act as a support for the floors and the roof above but also to strengthen the whole structure.

Most stone keeps had at least two or three floors. The lowest space was used for storage or as a dungeon although at first some seem to have been fully or partially filled with earth or spoil. A well was often dug (or the keep built around an existing one) so that there was always a supply of water during a siege. The entrance to the building would be made via steps up to the first floor where most had a large open hall in which the king or noble could receive guests and dispense justice. Above this or to one side would be their accommodation and a private chapel. Openings in the walls would have been limited, usually just enough to provide light and air. In some cases, a few round arched windows would have illuminated the hall and would have been closed off by wooden shutters at a time of trouble (most of the windows found today in castles were knocked through at a later date). Narrow passages were built through the walls with spiral staircases in the towers along the sides or corners. These gave access to the wall walk around the top of the walls which was both a look out and high point for attacking besiegers.

If the motte was to be retained as the key defensive feature of a castle but was not stable enough to support the weight of a mighty stone tower then an alternative was to erect a hollow,

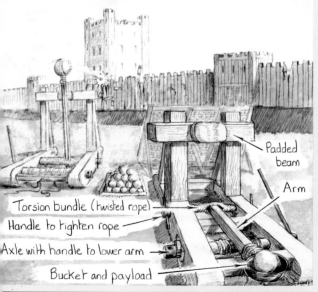

Torsion bundle (twisted rope)

Handle to tighten rope

Axle with handle to lower arm

Bucket and payload

Padded beam

Arm

FIG 3.6: Mangonel: This siege engine pictured here was the most basic form of stone throwing catapult which was likely to have been employed in medieval siege warfare. It used torsion (a force generated by twisting), in this case a bundle of rope, with the arm set within it so that as the axle was turned and the arm lowered down it twisted the bundle increasing the torsion. When it was released the arm sprung forward, hit the padded beam, and sent the projectile in the cup (or sling) flying out in a low trajectory probably reaching a target up to 100m (300ft) away.

circular shell keep. The motte was usually lowered in height and a high wall built around the top edge with a ring of wooden structures erected up against its inner face. The timber buildings inside could have provided similar spaces to those within a stone keep although they would have been very vulnerable to fire from flaming arrows shot over the walls and whipped up into flames by any wind blowing around its open interior. In some cases, a small shell keep or a stone tower was added to the outer walls around the castle when they were rebuilt in stone. These gave protection to a particular weak point around the defences, like a gateway.

Attacking stone keeps

Stone-throwing catapults, battering rams, and siege towers began to be used more widely by attacking forces during the 12th century. Just as castles were rebuilt in stone so new weapons

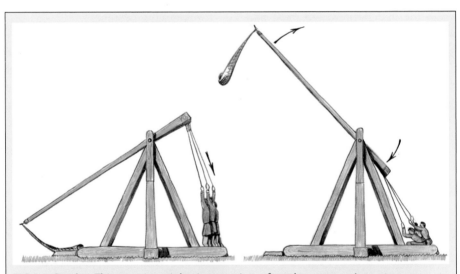

FIG 3.7: Perrier: This counterweight siege engine referred to as a perrier, petrary or beam sling mangonel had a pivoted arm, with the power to swing it coming from a group of men or women, probably from 5-15 in total depending upon the size of the machine (left). As they pulled down in unison (right) the long arm with the projectile was rapidly rotated, flicking the sling which gave the projectile an extra whip action to increase its velocity (in a similar way to a modern day tennis ball launcher for dogs enhances the action of the thrower's arm). These could reach further than a torsion mangonel, probably around 150m (450ft). They could be reloaded and fired quicker, and were lighter, making them more portable. It was a projectile hurled by one of these machines, believed to have been powered by an all-female team, which killed the father of Simon de Montfort, the Earl of Leicester during a siege at Toulouse in 1218.

Archers on the upper gallery give covering fire.

Attackers run across drawbridge onto battlements.

Siege tower pulled by oxen and manpower.

Ladders.

Fire resistant covering.

Embankment built across moat.

FIG 3.8: A siege tower or belfry was a tall timber structure which could either be a stationary platform to give attackers a better range of fire or a mobile structure with a drawbridge to enable them to get upon the battlements as shown here. They would have varied in size and design. This tall example has an upper gallery allowing archers to force back defenders as the men pour out onto the walls. These mobile towers would have been pulled and pushed by oxen or groups of men on wheels or rolled on logs, over an embankment across the moat made of bundles of branches and sticks in order to reach the walls. All the time it was being moved defenders would try and damage it with stones or set it alight with fire arrows, hence it needed to be covered in wet hides or other forms of sheeting to reduce the risk.

wealthiest nobles who had access to the knowledge and the funds to build such weapons and employ the specialists in siege warfare. However, they were so effective that even the most up-to-date stone castles could be forced to surrender before they were even unleashed. The largest weapons were often custom-made and built on site although some were dismantled after use and transported to another local castle where they could be stored until called upon again.

The first records implying the use of large machines which could hurl projectiles at the stone walls of castles are made in the late 12th and early 13th century. 'Petraries' are mentioned at King Richard's sieges of Nottingham and Marlborough in 1194. Prince Louis used mangonels at the siege of Dover Castle in 1216 (although these may have been more advanced trebuchets), and a request was made for wagons and materials for 'balistae' at the siege of Bedford Castle in 1224. However, without accurate drawings or descriptions relating to such references it is not clear the exact design of these machines. Therefore, much of the information about their form and how they worked comes from continental sources and later reconstructions made in the modern era.

and methods of undermining masonry walls were developed. It was usually only the King and a number of his

An early type of catapult used in the 12th century was the mangonel

31

FIG 3.9: In this image sappers (under the lean-to structure known as a sow or penthouse) have removed masonry from the corner of a tower and at the same time have inserted timbers to support the wall. They are now starting a fire in the gap which will give them time to escape before the supports burn through sending the wall above crashing down. Beneath the ground miners have dug a tunnel under another section of wall and are bringing through kindling in order to create a fire. This should create a gap above once the flames have burnt through the timbers or have cracked the foundations. Sometimes the defending castellan was invited to inspect works like this in the hope the garrison would surrender before the walls were destroyed. This was a crafty move as the successful attackers would then be the ones who would have to repair them.

(see FIG 3.6). The mangonel would have fired missiles at a relatively low trajectory so would have probably been used to smash timber and stone walls. Those which used a cup could also throw virtually any projectile including rocks, vessels filled with burning liquid, and diseased parts of animals or dead and mutilated human bodies.

Another type of throwing machine which seems to have proven popular by this period was the beam sling mangonel or perrier. These had a longer arm pivoted on a triangular frame with the end which held the projectile hanging over three to five times as far out as the other end. A sling which held the projectile was fixed at the tip with series of ropes attached to the short end. A large group of men or women, pulled the ropes together which rapidly swung the arm round until it hit a vertical beam where upon the sling gave an additional whip action as it released the projectile. A perrier could fire missiles a greater distance than the mangonel and at a higher trajectory so may have been used to knock off the tops of walls and towers and to hit buildings within the fortification.

Defenders always had a great advantage of height over the attackers. They could be more effective firing arrows and throwing projectiles from the top of the castle walls than those below could firing up. When Eustace de Vesci, a leading baron in the revolt against King John in 1216, was inspecting the siege of Barnard Castle, County Durham with the Scottish king Alexander II, he got too close to the castle walls and was shot dead by an archer. Therefore, to counter this, attackers built siege towers so they could improve their own advantage. Some seem to have been built like a counter castle, having a fixed timber tower as close to the walls as possible with a series of floors and ladders leading up to the open firing gallery on top. There may have been crenellations or a large shield with arrow slits to give those on top protection, while the front and sides of the structure itself could have been draped with hides to prevent defenders shooting fire arrows to burn it down. Other types of siege tower were designed to be mobile so they could be slowly moved up to the walls of the castle

with some type of drawbridge at the top lowered to bridge the gap to the battlements.

Although these siege engines were impressive and their presence alone may have been enough to force the garrison to surrender, there is little evidence that they ever brought down stone walls. For that the attackers turned to battering rams, sappers and miners. Battering rams made from a tree trunk with a metal head suspended under a protective canopy could be swung against a wall to try and force an opening. Although the timber gates were easier to break, that point was usually heavy fortified and guarded so rams would also have been used at potential weak points in the outer walls. Alternatively, a group of men under shields or some form of protective cover, would make their way up to the corner of a tower or wall and use picks and hammers to try and remove the masonry bit by bit (sapping). The wall was supported with props as they removed the masonry and then, when they had created a large enough gap, they would set fire to the timber supports to give them time to get away before the masonry wall came crashing down.

The most dramatic results though, came from mining. A tunnel was dug towards the castle walls by the attacking force, often employing

FIG 3.10: Hoarding: If an attack was imminent then there were additional features which could be added to the castle battlements to enhance its defensive capabilities. Hoarding was a timber shelter which projected out from the front edge of the wall, in this example at Caerphilly Castle, resting upon stout timbers set into sockets in the masonry. This gave defending archers better protection and space when shooting and allowed soldiers to drop hot sand, liquids, and stones down upon anyone trying to smash the walls. These would have been time consuming to construct so would have probably only been added to key points along the defences like gatehouses and towers.

specialist miners from Germany, with timber props supporting the cramped space as they approached their target. When they were under the masonry a large area could be dug out and kindling bundled up to fuel a fire which could either burn the props holding the stone wall up or create such heat that the foundations above cracked. The result was that a section of the castle wall or keep could collapse giving the attackers the opportunity to pour over the rubble and into the castle. The most notable example of this was during the siege of Rochester Castle by King John in 1216 when the entire corner of the keep was brought crashing down forcing the defenders to fall back behind the spine wall as a futile last line (see FIG 1.1.). Mining was a very slow process requiring specialist knowledge and soft ground and hence seems only to have been resorted to in a few major, long drawn-out sieges.

Defending stone keeps

Despite the formidable array of weaponry which could be brought to bear upon the new stone keeps and their castle walls, defenders still had a strong hand to play. For a start, the walls of many of these stone keeps were so thick that the sheer mass of stone, rubble and lime mortar could absorb the impact of heavy projectiles and remain partially intact when mined or sapped. In order to have a sound footing many stone keeps had been erected upon a foundation of solid rock which would prohibit mining under it. At the siege of Dover Castle, Prince Louis used miners to attack the outer walls of the fortification as the underlying geology was of soft chalk. However, the defenders realised what they were doing, dug their own counter tunnels and intercepted the attackers;

FIG 3.11: Scarborough Castle: William le Gros founded a castle on this high promontory above the Yorkshire town of Scarborough during the anarchy of King Stephen's reign. As with many built during this civil war he had not received royal permission so when Henry II took the throne in 1154 he demanded castles like Scarborough be handed to the crown. Le Gros initially resisted but when a royal army arrived at the door he handed his timber fortification to the new king and it was Henry who built the great stone keep which is today partially ruined due to events 500 years later (see FIG 7.1).

FIG 3.12. Ludlow Castle: This impressive castle built at one end of a ridge above the River Teme was constructed in stone when it was begun in the 1090s, with the material dug out of the defensive ditches used to build the masonry walls. It was besieged by King Stephen in 1139 during which defenders threw over a large hook on a rope, called a crow, which managed to catch the Scottish Prince Henry who was an ally of the English crown. It was only thanks to quick action by Stephen that prevented them managing to haul him up over the battlements (they could have used him for ransom or as a bargaining tool to end the siege). It was in the decades after that event that the great stone keep in the right of this picture was built on the site of the original gatehouse, when the castle was expanded and a new outer bailey formed.

the remains of these can still be seen today. Although miners would seem to have the upper hand as they were digging out of sight, defenders soon realised that a pan filled with water placed on the ground would ripple when they were close to the foundations giving them an early warning and the chance to dig their own counter mines or to prepare to fill any gaps which appeared in the walls.

An additional advantage for the defenders was that the mangonels, battering rams and siege towers were

FIG 3.13. Conisbrough Castle: Most stone keeps and towers built in the 12th century were square in plan but a few like Orford, Suffolk and here at Conisbrough, Yorks built in the 1180s had a circular core. It was designed to be an imposing private retreat for the owner Hamelin de Warenne, Earl of Surrey, with space behind its very thick walls for just a hall and a couple of private chambers. However, militarily the design had potential weak points as the six buttresses which create its cog like plan had square corners. These could be undermined and there were limited arrow loops for defenders to cover those points. It only faced one notable siege in 1317 when the owner John de Warenne kidnapped the wife of Thomas, Earl of Lancaster, who he blamed for blocking his divorce in the law courts. In retaliation, the Earl besieged and took Conisbrough Castle, only for him to lose it to the crown after he tried to overthrow Edward II a few years later.

use during this period had a limited distance they could be effective from, so had to be fairly close to the walls, keeping them within range of defenders firing flaming arrows. The timber structure of towers and battering rams would probably have been covered in wet hides or similar materials in an effort to reduce the chance of them catching fire, but many must have gone up in an inferno of flames trapping men on the uppermost floor. Battering rams and sappers were very vulnerable to being damaged or maimed from materials dropped upon them from the castle battlements. Stones, flaming substances, hot sand, lime, and other dangerous projectiles could set fire to protective covers, burn the skin or even kill the men beneath them. Rams could also be countered by lowering large padded mats down over the walls to soften the impact of the metal ram's head while men with grappling hooks would try and grab the end and disable it. Mangonels and perriers were also used by defenders who could site them on top of towers. The extra height would allow them to reach further than those used by attackers below and they were mainly used to take out the enemy's siege engines. As they were relatively simple to operate, they could be powered by groups of non-military men or women who otherwise would be of little use to the defence of a castle.

made of timber, so defenders could try and set fire to these stationary or lumbering weapons. The catapults in

FIG 3.14: Castle Rising, Norfolk: The magnificent Norman keep at Castle Rising was built in the years after 1138 by William d'Aubigny II. Its large size reflected his new-found wealth and was designed both for defence and as a hunting lodge with a rectangular plan and a cross wall dividing the interior. The entrance on the first floor was covered by a forebuilding which housed the stone steps (pictured here) leading up to a waiting chamber. It not only provided an extra level of defence but also made a grand entrance for any of William's guests.

FIG 3.15: The Tower of London: This most famous of Norman stone keeps was erected by William the Conqueror from the late 1070s. The huge structure with its distinctive square form, shallow buttresses and round arched openings was originally given a whitewash finish to protect the stonework and mortar from water and frost damage. Hence, it became known as the White Tower, after which the whole castle is named. It is likely that through the medieval period many similar castle structures were painted in this way, possibly with splashes of bright colours to highlight some features.

CURTAIN WALLED CASTLES
Towers, Moats and Trebuchets

Castles in the mid-13th century

King Henry III was only nine when he ascended the throne during the First Barons' War and he relied upon senior ministers to rule on his behalf until finally taking complete control after another rebellion in 1232. Henry spent time and money on his castles in this country but his foreign expeditions were a failure and discontent with his rule once again encouraged barons to rise up and force him in 1258 to agree to a reform of his government under the Provisions of Oxford. Henry, like John before him, tried to annul them and soon the country was at war again in the Second Barons' War. This time under the leadership of Simon de Montfort, the rebels captured the King and his heir Edward, but the young prince managed to escape and the royal forces defeated de Montfort at the Battle of Evesham in 1265. It took a couple of years for Henry to regain full control and take castles which still held out for the rebels, and by the time he died in 1272 reforms had been passed which resulted in relatively stable government.

In the wake of sieges during the Barons' War with King John and Prince Louis's invasion, castle designers began to respond to the threat posed by the new siege engines and tactics of undermining walls. The damage caused during the conflict was repaired, at Rochester a new form of tower replaced the original square one which had been destroyed by mining (FIG 1.1) and at Dover the gateway which had been penetrated by Louis's forces was blocked up and a new enhanced entrance built to reinforce this perpetual weak point. Across the country new keeps and towers were built with battered plinths, which involved an angled face at the bottom of the wall. This made a potentially vulnerable point thicker and would help deflect the blows from a battering ram. It also allowed any projectile dropped from the battlements to be thrown outwards after hitting the sloping surface, posing more of a threat to approaching soldiers. Round towers rather than square ones became the standard form as they had no weak corners to be undermined and were better at resisting the impact from a stone missile.

FIG 4.1: The siege of Kenilworth Castle in 1266, pictured here, was probably the longest and most expensive ever undertaken in medieval Britain. The barons had once again rebelled against their monarch, in this case John's son Henry III, and under their leader Simon de Montfort they had defeated the King at Lewes in 1264 and taken him and his son, the future Edward I, prisoner. However, the young prince escaped and led the royal forces to victory the following year at Evesham where Simon de Montfort was brutally killed and the King released. In the wake of this defeat, the surviving rebel forces of just over a thousand men took refuge in de Montfort's castle at Kenilworth in Warwickshire and refused to hand it over to the Crown. So in summer 1266 Henry surrounded this mighty fortification, which had been upgraded by his father with a strong curtain wall and towers surrounded by a vast water-filled moat. The siege lasted around six months with the King's forces building siege towers, mounting an attack by boat and pounding the walls and interior with the latest stone-throwing machines to such an intensity at one point that the projectiles were said to have smashed into each other in mid-air. Yet all these failed and they had to wait it out until disease and shortages of food forced the garrison to surrender in December.

At the same time there was a change in the overall approach to the design of castles. The focus in this country up to this point had been making a single stronghold which the garrison could retreat back to if the outer walls failed. Now the emphasis shifted into making the outer walls much stronger so that the enemy could not get past them in the first place. To achieve this the new curtain walls, as they are known, were built taller than earlier defences to help neutralise the threat from stone throwing machines. They had round towers placed at regular intervals around the perimeter which now protruded further out to ensure defenders had a complete range of fire along the base of the walls. The gateway could also be enhanced by building it between two large towers (mural towers) with not just a gate but a series of barriers which attackers would have to pass through. The

FIG 4.2: Framlingham Castle, Suffolk: This was one of the earliest castles built with curtain walls and no internal stronghold. It was erected by Roger Bigod, the Earl of Norfolk, from 1189. Its tall, stone wall ring set around the outer edge of a raised earthwork and surrounded by a moat made a formidable barrier which would have limited the effectiveness of siege engines. The wall was interrupted at regular intervals by 13 square-planned, open-backed towers which originally had removable gangways rather than a solid floor so if the enemy managed to get onto the wall walk they would find themselves trapped between each one. The fighting gallery on top of the towers was accessed by ladders and would allow defenders to fire arrows and crossbow bolts down upon anyone trying to undermine the wall outside and those had broken through into the interior of the castle. Despite this cutting edge castle technology, the fortification surrendered after only three days when King John surrounded it in March 1216 without putting the defences to the test. It may be that because of John's formidable reputation following his destruction of Rochester Castle only five months earlier, that Roger did not want the same thing to happen to his new castle and ordered his garrison to stand down.

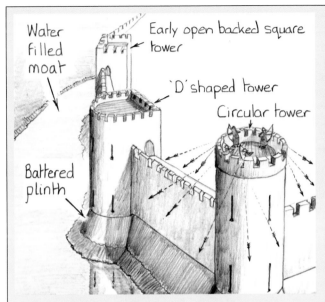

FIG 4.3: A drawing of a section of a curtain walled castle. Unlike earlier fortifications where the towers were absent or were just added at irregular points these new fortifications had mural towers (towers within a walled structure rather than freestanding) positioned at regular intervals. The earlier type with a square plan and an open back is shown in the background, the same form as used at Framlingham. In the mid and foreground are a 'D' shaped and round tower which are distinctive of later castles built from the 13th century. Note that the combination of the fighting gallery at the top and the carefully positioned arrow loops in the walls of the towers now allowed defenders to have a full range of fire upon enemy soldiers who were attacking the base of the wall, had got onto the wall walk or had broken through the gates (as indicated by the arrows in the foreground).

reinforced by being surrounded by a deep moat, where possible filled with water so it would be difficult for enemy miners to dig beneath without flooding their tunnels. The advantage of this design was that it freed the enclosed space within the stone walls, referred to as a ward, for any size of building, allowing the king or noble to build themselves a large hall and fine accommodation worthy of their status. The first of these new curtain walled castles appeared from the middle of the 12th century but they were not always successful and it was only during the next century that the designs were perfected.

Attacking a Curtain Walled Castle

The improved defences of these 13th-century curtain walled castles now posed a major obstacle to attackers to which they responded with ever more powerful weapons. The latest in stone-throwing engines was the trebuchet. It was similar to the smaller perrier with a long wooden arm swinging in an 'A' frame with a sling at the far end.

FIG 4.4: Strengthening the gateway of a curtain walled castle was essential to making the design work. Rather than just building a large single structure with the entrance below, the new gateways usually had a pair of round or 'D' shaped towers built either side of a narrow passageway. These projecting towers with numerous arrow loops allowed defenders to fire at approaching attackers from an angle so they could get under their covers or shields and then when they were closer they could rain projectiles down upon them from either side. If they got past these then the drawbridge lifted out of the way to block the gateway, leaving the moat and in some cases a pit on the other side to try and cross. Behind this would be a mighty portcullis shod in iron, strong enough to halt their approach but with the added danger that defenders could fire through the timber grid to slow their progress. Even if they managed to get past this and reach the main gates they would still have to survive the onslaught of projectiles and red hot sand dropped through murder holes or meurtrières in the ceiling (although these were often used by defenders to pour water down to put out fires set up against the timber gates).

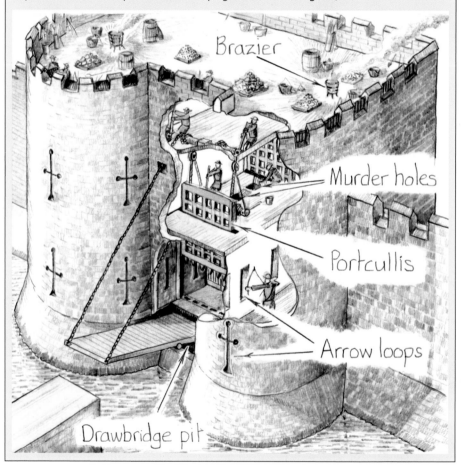

Brazier

Murder holes

Portcullis

Arrow loops

Drawbridge pit

FIG 4.5: The gaps which the portcullis ran down, rectangular holes in the ceiling above and arrow loops along the side of the passageway can be found in ruined castles , as with these examples, to remind us how treacherous the approach would have been for attackers

FIG 4.6: Trebuchet: This was one of the few siege engines which was not based on Roman machines but instead seems to have developed in the Middle East before the mid-12th century. The first use in this country was probably by Prince Louis during his invasion of England in 1215. At one end was a sling in which the stone ball was held, which ran within a grooved slot in the base of the frame to help it maintain an accurate line as it

was fired. The stone balls usually weighed between 40-100kg (90-220lbs) and could be thrown a distance of 300-400 yards which could keep larger types out of the reach of archers defending the castle. When Henry III was besieging Kenilworth Castle, Warwickshire (FIG 4.1) the original trebuchets were being hit by defenders so he ordered larger types from as far away as the south coast so they could be positioned further back. At the other end of the arm was a large counterweight, a pivoted wooden box filled with metal, sand, or stones to create a mass weighing a number of tons (the range of the machine was probably changed by reducing or increasing the weight in the counter end, using an alternative size ball or releasing the projectile at a different point). The English army stripped the lead off churches for the counterweights of their trebuchets when invading Scotland in the late 13th century. As these siege engines could throw projectiles high into the interior of the castle, more gruesome objects like severed heads to demoralise the garrison, or rotting animals to spread disease were used.

FIG 4.7: Crossbows

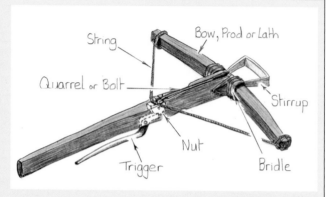

Crossbows came into widespread use during the 12th century. Their powerful action and heavy bolts, often referred to in medieval times as quarrels, could pierce chain mail and armour so were regarded as unchivalrous but various attempts to ban them by the Pope and later in the Magna Carta fell on deaf ears. Richard the Lionheart died from gangrene after he was struck by a crossbow bolt while besieging Chalus, France. The bow, also known as a prod or lath, was originally made from a single piece of wood and is referred to as a self or single bow. Composite crossbows made by laminating strips of horn and sinew onto a wooden core were available from the mid-12th century and the extra energy that this could store meant that the bow could be shorter, making them ideal for use on horseback. Both of these types were gradually replaced by steel during the early 15th century. The strings were usually made from braided cord or fabric, hemp, linen or sinew which on early types were pulled back (spanning) by hand and then held by a locking mechanism before they were fired. Types of crossbows with stirrups to take one or both feet to aid loading, were developed during the 13th century. The Samson or spanning belt was a useful tool, which hooked the string to the crossbowman or arbalist's waist so with the bow held underfoot as they stood up it stretched the string back. Later mechanisms using levers, pulleys and winches were used on ever more powerful crossbows which could hit targets over 400 yards away. As the operator did not need strong arms to pull the string back it meant that the old, young and infirm could operate one whereas it took longer to train and attain the required strength to be an effective archer. Crossbowmen on the besieging force had to carry a tall shield called a pavise to crouch behind while they were reloading.

The crossbow became an important weapon in siege warfare. In 1224 Henry III is recorded as ordering 15,000 bolts from Corfe Castle in Dorset, out of a total of three times that number, for his siege of the rebellious Falkes de Breauté's Bedford Castle. The King lost around 200 men to the weapons of the defenders but using a combination of stone throwing machines, mining and all-out attack, they were finally able to break through the defences after eight weeks. Henry showed little mercy and had around 80 men from the garrison hanged, an unusually ruthless act for this period. Falkes's name lived on at one of his estates in south London where 'Falkes Hall' later became Vauxhall. The motor company of the same name which is based in one of his old medieval manors in Luton, still uses the de Breauté griffin on its cars.

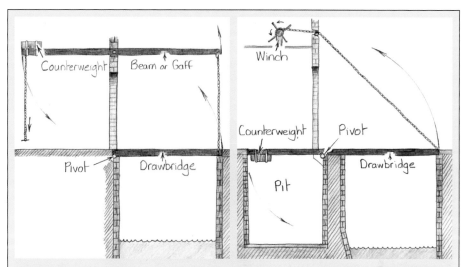

FIG 4.8: The Drawbridge: Earlier castles might have had a fixed bridge across a ditch with a section which could be lifted out at a time of war or removed as an enemy approached. The familiar lifting drawbridge became common by the early 13th century. Some may have been a small bridge hinged at the base and pulled up by chains but this would require great effort if the bridge was of a larger size. Hence some had a pair of counterweighted arms above (left) which were connected to the bridge by chains with the counterweighted end pulled down to lift the bridge up (very much like a canal lift bridge). Alternatively, the drawbridge could be pivoted near the middle with a counterweight fitted to the end above a pit (right) so the chains lifting the far end required minimal effort to raise it up. The advantage of the latter was that the deep pit made yet another hazard for attackers to try and cross if they managed to hack their way through the timber bridge.

However, rather than using people as the counterweight on the short end the trebuchet had a large pivoted timber box filled with stone, sand or other materials which could weigh a couple of tons. The long sling end was pulled or winched down which raised the heavy counterweight end. Then as the trigger cord was pulled the arm swung round and threw the projectile with much greater force and accuracy than the earlier machines. The high trajectory it produced was probably more effective in smashing the battlements or damaging buildings within the castle rather than smashing into the face of the curtain walls. One of the largest made in this country was the War Wolf, built for Edward I's siege of Stirling Castle. It took a team of carpenters around three months to build and had to be transported around the coast and then over land until it could be set up in front of the Scottish fortification. Although the

FIG 4.9: Moats: Perhaps the most iconic part of a medieval castle was the moat. Its waters reflected its walls and battlements with the drawbridge the only point where it could be crossed. Most castles had a deep ditch around them which was originally formed where the material was dug to make the banks behind it. In many locations these were left dry as it was not possible to fill them with water either because the fortifications were too high above a good source or the ground was unsuitable. In most early castles a deep muddy ditch was regarded as formidable enough defence although some could be lined with spikes or thorns as a further deterrent. Water-filled moats became more common from the 13th century, especially after their success at Kenilworth. Not only were they hard to cross but they also provided a defence against mining since any tunnel dug towards the walls could cave in and be flooded when trying to pass under it. In peaceful times the moat could also act as a fishpond providing the garrison with another source of food. In the later Middle Ages new castles, better described as fortified manor houses as here at Kirby Muxloe Castle, Leics, were built in low-lying areas where they could easily have wet moats filled by neighbouring rivers and they became a must-have fashionable feature through into the Tudor period.

Scots surrendered before it had been fired the King was so keen to use his new weapon that he would not accept it until he had tried the huge trebuchet out on their defences.

As the finest castles now had stone walls with battered plinths, water-filled moats, and projecting round towers so the base of the wall could be well covered by archers, so battering rams and mining became less effective. The gateway was a potential weak point but if there had been time for the defenders to bar the gates shut, lower the portcullis and lift the drawbridge then targeting this point would have been wasted energy. Siege towers were still an important weapon as they took away the defenders height advantage and fixed ones were built during some sieges with archers and possibly a stone-throwing machine on top to target a section of wall. Older castles without such defences could still be breached by portable siege towers and ladders with hooks at the top to cling onto the battlements as men rushed up them. The weaponry used by attackers more often than not seems to have been effective more in the terror from the pounding of the stones upon walls and or the threat of what they could unleash rather than in their actual destructive capabilities. As the siege at Kenilworth showed, strong defences and a wily leader could hold off an attack made using all the weapons and tactics the attacking King and his son had available.

FIG 4.10: For the defenders there was a variety of positions from which to shoot both arrows and crossbow bolts. Arrow loops could be simple vertical slits (left), have a splayed base (centre left) so it was easier for archers to shoot targets closer to the walls, or have a cross shape (centre right and right).

CONCENTRIC WALLED CASTLES
Ballista and Machicolations

Edward I's Welsh Castles

When Edward I ascended the throne after the death of his father in 1272 he began to look around Britain for new acquisitions, and during his reign spent huge sums of money and time trying to gain control of Wales and Scotland. In order to mount a campaign against Scotland he would first need to pacify the Welsh so they could not outflank his forces when he later headed north. The territory along much of the border and throughout South Wales was controlled by semi-independent Marcher lords while the mountainous area of Mid and North Wales was under the control of Llywelyn ap Gruffydd, who since 1267 had been recognised by the English King as the Prince of Wales. Llywelyn though, had made it clear that his allegiances lay elsewhere and he infuriated Edward when he refused to pay homage to him at Chester in 1275 and married Eleanor de Montfort, the daughter of Simon who had nearly overthrown the English throne a decade earlier. Edward paid pirates to seize Llywelyn's wife when she sailed from France to meet her husband

and then raised a massive army to invade his principality of Gwynedd in a pincer movement with one force attacking along the North Wales coast while another landed in Anglesey and destroyed the harvest. This deprived Llywelyn's army of food and forced him to the negotiating table where upon he lost much of his territory but was permitted to retain his land west of Conwy and finally meet his new bride. The harsh terms imposed upon the Welsh caused deep resentment, such that in 1282 Llywelyn's brother Dafydd initiated a rebellion forcing Edward to invade once again.

Although the English King used the same tactics as before, this time his force on Anglesey were routed when they tried to cross the Menai Straits. After a further defeat Edward's invasion looked in trouble, but luckily for him Llywelyn was killed a few weeks later after a deception and ambush by Marcher lords who had promised to pay homage to him. With Llywelyn gone Welsh resistance cracked and Edward conquered the remaining territory and began the construction of a ring of new castles

FIG 5.1: Caernarfon Castle was built by Edward I as one of a ring of fortifications designed to enable the invading English to maintain a firm grip upon power in North Wales. It was an expensive and time-consuming project with Caernarfon alone costing far more than the most important English castles like Dover, partly because Edward intended it to be the capital of the region. Its impressive walls, towers and gateways manned by around 30-40 men during peacetime (most castles would only have a handful of armed men) was put to the test a number of times. This view shows an attack by Owain Glyndŵr in 1403 when his Welsh supporters backed by French soldiers almost broke through the castle's defences.

so he could retain a strong grip upon the land.

He first sought to tighten his grip on the part of North Wales which he took from Llywelyn after the first invasion in 1277 by erecting new castles. These included Flint – on the Dee Estuary and Rhuddlan, where he had the River Clwyd dredged and straightened, in both cases so ships could reach them if they were besieged by land. At the conclusion of the second invasion of 1282 the King set about building a further four castles to suppress the remaining part of North Wales at Conwy, Caernarfon, Harlech and Beaumaris. At Conwy Edward removed the old Welsh monastery which occupied this strategically important position and built a new curtain walled castle upon a rocky outcrop overlooking the river estuary. Caernarfon Castle was the most ambitious of Edward's fortifications as he intended this site

FIG 5.2: Flint Castle, Flintshire: This was the first of Edward's Welsh castles begun in 1277 on the banks of the Dee Estuary. It had a unique plan with curtain walls surrounding the inner ward which featured round towers and a tall, freestanding circular planned keep, in the foreground of this view. This had thick walls up to 7m (23ft) deep which could both protect the gateway and provide a last line of defence if the castle fell. The constable of the castle was forced to set fire to it during the 1294 rebellion to save it falling into Welsh hands, although it was later rebuilt.

FIG 5.3: Rhuddlan Castle, Denbighshire: Built at the same time as Flint, Rhuddlan had a diamond-shaped inner ward with a pair of large gatehouses at opposing corners and a low outer wall forming its concentric defences. Edward had the River Clwyd below dredged and straightened so that ships could bring supplies up during a siege.

to be the administrative centre of the region. The narrow site beside the junction of the River Seiont and the Menai Straits resulted in a similar design to that at Conwy except its towers were polygonal and the walls built with bands of different colours in an attempt by the king to link his work to that of the Romans who had established a fort nearby.

A new development in castle design was introduced at a number of castles, most notably Caerphilly Castle in South Wales, which used concentric walls. In these new fortifications the concept of focusing the defences upon a strong curtain wall was extended to make two rings of masonry rather than one. The inner wall would be much higher than the outer so that archers on the tall battlements could

51

FIG 5.4: Conwy Castle: This mighty fortification set on a rocky outcrop above the River Conwy was built in the 1280s along with a walled town to the north west. Because of the limitations of the site its tall walls and mural towers were around the crest of the ridge with the inner ward (right) separated from the outer ward (left) by a gatehouse and drawbridge. The main gateway was on the western town end and another accessed the river at the other end so again the castle could be supplied from the river if besieged by land.

fire over the top of the lower resulting in double the firepower directed towards a besieging army outside. If an attacking force managed to get through the first line of defences then they would find themselves trapped in a narrow open strip between the two walls, a potential killing field where they could be massacred by arrow fire from both the inner and outer walls.

It was at Harlech where Edward was able to build a compact, squared-planned castle with these new concentric defences. It was set upon a rocky outcrop overlooking Cardigan Bay with steep slopes and a deep ditch creating a formidable barrier around the fortification. Within this were the lower outer line and a tall inner wall with round towers in the corners. As Harlech Castle was built upon solid rock mining would be impractical and an attack over the walls would have been suicidal if the castle was fully manned. The only weak point was the entrance on a level ground to the east but this was marked by a mighty gatehouse set between two 'D' shaped towers with three portcullises, two sets of gates

Dungeons

Iron doors leading to dark and dank underground chambers or trap doors in the top of bottle-shaped cells (oubliettes) where the wretched were supposedly thrown and tortured are the highlight of many castle tours. Unfortunately, most medieval castles were never built with dungeons and many of those today which are assumed to be as such turn out to be store rooms or medieval toilets. In the Middle Ages there was little need for prisons. If an important person was held they would usually be kept in a secure room high in a tower or keep. Defeated enemy soldiers were either released or killed, and the only time an underground cell might be filled is when holding a criminal before a trial. It was not until the early 17th century that, with growing opposition to the widespread use of the death penalty the idea of prison as a punishment for petty crime developed and castles were ideally placed to be converted for this use.

and a drawbridge. As with Edward's other Welsh castles he ensured they had access to the sea, in this case with a set of steps leading down to a water gate at the foot of the cliffs

where the sea originally lapped. The value of this was proven in the winter of 1294-95 when a rebellion led by Madog ap Llywelyn resulted in many of the new castles being besieged and despite only having around 40 men at one point Harlech held out thanks to food being delivered from Ireland via its water gate.

As a result of Madog's rebellion the King sought to further strengthen his military grip on the country and made building a new castle on Anglesey, overlooking the Menai Straits, a priority. With no restrictions upon the design from this flat, virgin site at Beaumaris, a symmetrical, concentric walled castle was planned with a moat around its lower outer walls. On its southern side a sea dock was dug out protected by a tall wall for archers and on the other side the main gateway into the outer ward. The huge cost of building meant that work progressed in fits and starts and when it finally ceased in 1330 the castle was still not complete to its

FIG 5.5: Harlech Castle: Its tall inner walls, corner towers and gatehouse (right) overshadow the lower outer wall (in the foreground) which together form the formidable concentric defences.

FIG 5.6: Caerphilly Castle, South Wales: Perhaps the finest of all medieval castles in Britain, second only in size to Windsor, but unlike that Royal castle Caerphilly is principally all of one date. It is the first true concentric castle, built for the ambitious Gilbert de Clare, Lord of Glamorgan, during the early 1270s to prevent the Welsh leader Llywelyn invading South Wales. In addition to its two rings of mighty walls and towers Gilbert also built dams to create lakes around his fortification (as had proven effective at Kenilworth a decade earlier) and designed the main gatehouse so it could be defended as an independent structure should the rest of the castle fall into enemy hands.

intended height, yet it made for one of the most perfect medieval military designs.

Attacking and Defending Castles in the late 13th century

For an attacking force the concentric walls, moats and powerful gatehouses made a well prepared and manned castle virtually unassailable. However, there were still tactics, used in the past, which could be an effective way of forcing defenders into submission. Stone throwing machines might not be able to knock the new walls down but their constant pounding and the threat that they could flatten the buildings inside the castle could have a significant psychological effect. When Edward's forces attacked Dolforwyn Castle

FIG 5.7: Beaumaris Castle, Anglesey: Like Caerphilly, Beaumaris marks the high point in the design of medieval castles. Although it was never fully completed or its fortifications truly tested, you can still see how effective its defences would have been when fully manned. Most armies would have struggled to get across the water filled moat, then penetrate the low and high concentric walls and towers behind it whilst being shot at from all angles (note the arrow loops at the base of the wall to shoot those approaching under a cover or shield). This view shows how the tall inner and low outer walls of its concentric design allowed archers and crossbowmen on both walls to fire down upon the enemy.

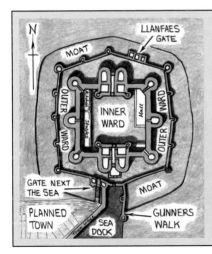

FIG 5.8: A plan of Beaumaris Castle showing the concentric walls with its towers and large gatehouses all surrounded by a water filled moat. The dock on the southern side could be protected by archers on the high wall along its eastern side so protecting this vital access for ships bringing supplies.

55

FIG 5.9: A drawing showing how concentric low and high walls enabled archers to create double the fire power at approaching soldiers. It was also important that the space between the walls, the outer ward, was compact limiting the enemy's movement and enabling defenders to fire on them from both sides. In the most advanced castles like Caerphilly there were numerous passages and staircases which allowed for the rapid movement of troops to any part of the castle.

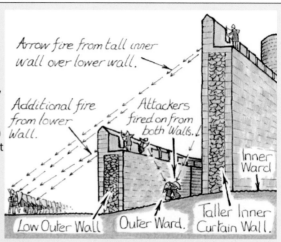

Arrow fire from tall inner wall over lower wall.

Additional fire from lower Wall.

Attackers fired on from both Walls.

Inner Ward

Low Outer Wall

Outer Ward.

Taller Inner Curtain Wall.

in 1277 his siege engines damaged the corners of the keep and curtain wall (over 50 stone balls were found during excavations) and although the men inside surrendered after ten days claiming they had a lack of water, the pounding of the projectiles may have had some part to play.

Nor did they always send large rocks flying up but sometimes used showers of smaller stones which could rain down like exploding shrapnel. At Dryslwyn Castle these smaller stone balls were discovered during excavations along with large ones hewn by quarrymen. The threat from a powerful new siege engine might intimidate a garrison to surrender, and especially if it was given a threatening name could force them to panic and open the gates. The most effective method however still seems to have been to

surround the castle and starve out the occupants. A lack of food, water and the spread of disease within the tight confines of the castle walls often forced the besieged to surrender and is why Edward made such a point of protecting the access to river or sea for his Welsh castles. Not only was the taking of the castle important to the attacking commander but the ransoming of captured nobles and the sacking of the castle and its associated settlement might bring rich rewards for the king and his mercenaries who might choose to take loot in lieu of payment. When Edward I forced Edinburgh Castle to surrender after an intense, three-day bombardment he pillaged the site and took most of its treasured riches back with him to England.

The defenders of the new castles built in this period had many advantages.

FIG 5.10: Longbows: This detail from a famous medieval illustration of the Battle of Crécy in 1346 from Jean Froissart's Chronicles showing the French on the left with crossbows and the English on the right with longbows. The former had long been a very effective weapon for the defences of castles alongside more conventional short bows. The exact origins of the long bow are unknown but the Welsh armies had perfected its use and after the conquest of Wales it was adopted by the English. In its fully developed form it was 1.8 - 2.1m (6' - 6'10') long (although shorter bows might be classified as a longbow) made from yew, ash or elm (usually yew), with strings made from hemp, linen, silk, sinew or rawhide and attached at the top and bottom by nocks, often made from the tip of an animal horn. They were very powerful weapons able to fire a greater distance than crossbows, around 230m (251 yards), the length of two football pitches end on, although even longer distances are recorded. Arrows could be shot at a rate of up to 12 per a minute and some were available which could pierce armour making this one of the most lethal medieval weapons. However, it took great skill and strength to fire and longbowmen's skeletons are recognisable due to the extra bone which developed in one arm and defects in their shoulders and wrists. Its principal use was on the battlefield where it could be fired high to rain arrows down upon the enemy but it was also used in the defence and attack of castles during the 14th and 15th century alongside short bows and crossbows.

Deception

As castle defences became ever more advanced so other methods of attack were used. The Scots under Robert the Bruce could not match the English for siege engines so they used deception to take a number of castles; a clever solution which limited the loss of life and saved a fortune on machinery. At Linlithgow Castle in 1313 the Bruce sent a local merchant up to the castle with a cart piled full of hay. As he was let in the cart stopped in the castle gateway so it could not be shut. The Scots then stormed the castle and massacred the garrison inside. The English obviously did not learn from this mistake as less than 30 years later the Scots played the same trick again, in Edinburgh. This time they dressed up as merchants selling supplies and managed to block the gates so their forces hiding nearby could rush into the castle. One night, at Roxburgh in 1314, a number of Bruce's men threw black cloaks over themselves and approached the castle on all fours so the defenders in the dim light thought they were grazing cattle. When a few got close enough they threw off their cloaks and scaled the walls and threw open the gates so the rest of their force could take the castle.

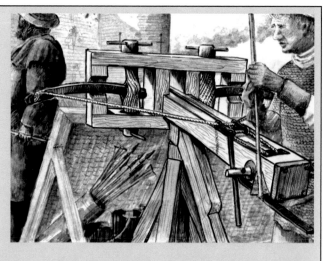

FIG 5.11: Ballista: Large mounted crossbows, usually referred to as ballista, could vary in size from a compact version illustrated here to giant machines with bows up to 5 or 6m (15-18ft). They begin to appear in records from the early 14th century although they may have been used earlier. Some had a large single bow mounted on a huge frame, others were based on the Roman ballistae having two separate arms fixed in twisted rope (like the mangonel). This latter device also known as a springald (illustrated here) was set within a frame with the string pulled back by a hook and ropes wound up by handles at the rear and then held ready to fire by a nut (as on the crossbow). A large arrow or bolt up to 5ft long was then placed in the slot and the trigger underneath pulled to fire it. Examples have been reconstructed which have had a range of up to 300-400m (328-437 yards) and were so powerful they could pierce a number of soldiers in one shot. Although they could be used by attacking armies most ballista or springalds were mounted on the castle's walls and the threat of being skewered by one of its bolts would have been enough to make soldiers think twice about approaching it's defences.

The walls were generally higher than earlier fortifications, making it harder for trebuchets to hurl stones into the inside of the castle. Towers were numerous to cover all lengths of the defences and also deeper so there was room for siege engines to be positioned on top. Not only are stone-throwing devices believed to have been used in these locations but there are also records showing that ballista, a type of giant crossbow, were being positioned on the battlements from the early 14th century if not before.

Cranes
There was a variety of devices used by defenders to either grab attackers or their weapons or to drop incendiary devices or rocks down upon their heads. Large hooks on ropes or poles, devices which could grab the end of battering rams and cranes which could be swung out from the battlements to drop heavy objects below could have all been used. In 1319 the Flemish engineer John Crabbe designed for the Scots, who were defending Berwick from the English, bales of wood bound by iron which were covered in pitch and set alight, then swung out on cranes and dropped on the cover used by English sappers, setting the sow alight and causing the men to retreat. A similar trick was performed at a later date at Berwick when defenders swung out blazing bundles only for the wind to suddenly change and blow the flames back into the town setting it on fire.

FIG 5.12: Machicolations: A view looking up at the parapet and crenellations supported on stone brackets (corbels) which created a gap through which defenders could drop all manner of hot substances and rocks down upon soldiers attacking the base of the walls. These machicolations are distinctive of 14th- and 15th-century work and were favoured by architects on mock castles in the 18th and 19th century.

Around the same time, it became common for a row of projecting stone corbels (brackets) to be built around the top of castles so that the battlements could project outwards from the wall below. This feature called machicolations was in effect a permanent type of hoarding which had gaps below through which red hot sand, boiling water or stones could be dropped on the enemy below.

Edward I's Scottish Campaign

After King Alexander III of Scotland died following a riding accident in

FIG 5.13: Dunnottar Castle, Aberdeenshire: This dramatic clifftop castle was according to legend captured by William Wallace in 1297 during the Scottish Wars of Independence, and its garrison marched into the church and burnt alive. The English attempted to refortify the ruins in 1336 as a forward base for a new invasion but the Scots again captured it later that year and destroyed its defences. The buildings which survive today mostly date from the 15th and 16th century.

1286, his only heir, the three-year-old Margaret was living in Norway, so the Guardians of Scotland were established to rule the kingdom. King Edward I was in the process of arranging the marriage of his son to the infant queen which would potentially stabilise this troublesome border when Margaret tragically fell ill and died on the journey to Scotland in 1290. With the risk of civil war between competing Scottish nobles vying for the crown, Edward was invited to arbitrate and when John Balliol was chosen the English King ensured that the Scots were his feudal vassals and had to pay towards the upkeep of English defences and military campaigns. The Scottish nobles quickly grew tired of the situation and negotiated the Auld Alliance with the French who were at war with the English at the time. In retaliation, Edward invaded Scotland in 1296 in the first of a series of attempts by him to subjugate the country during which his army besieged and captured a number of Scottish castles before they were frequently recaptured by the Scots. Edward never succeeded in totally conquering the country and after his death on the way to another campaign north of the border in 1307 his son, Edward II failed as a military leader and at Bannockburn seven years later Robert the Bruce defeated the English and established himself as the Scottish King.

Although the possession of key castles had played their part in the wars, the campaigns had been settled by open battle. As the 14th century progressed it would be tactical warfare across the countryside rather than the control of fortified positions which would become increasingly important. The military significance of castles in Britain had begun its steady decline. However, with the Welsh always keen to revolt and the Scots making regular raids into the north of the England castles of all sizes would remain critical along these border regions.

TOWER HOUSES AND COASTAL FORTS

Gatehouses, Gunpowder and Cannon

The End of the Castle

For around 250 years, civil war, invasions and local disputes in Britain had centred around castles, but from the early 14th century they began to lose their military value. Part of the reason for this was a relative stability within England. No longer were the King and his nobility threatened by native Saxons or rebellious barons, now there was structure to the kingdom and a fledgling parliament to reign in the monarch's excesses. The Kings who were brought up speaking French, with Latin for the church and possibly German so they could converse with mercenaries, began to learn English and Henry IV, who came to the throne in 1399 was the first who spoke it as his native tongue. There was still the potential for trouble from pretenders to the throne if the King was seen as weak or had a lack of success on the battlefield. The crown had been disputed ever since King Richard II had ascended the throne in 1377 and

after he was deposed by the Duke of Lancaster, who became King Henry IV, there was the potential for the issue to boil over into conflict.

This was exactly what happened as his grandson, King Henry VI, under whom the Hundred Years War with France (1337-1453) had been lost resulting in a financial crisis, was increasingly viewed as weak and ineffectual. Richard, Duke of York, who also had a strong claim to the throne, took the opportunity to stake his claim and in a series of battles from 1455-85, the crown passed between the supporters of the Houses of Lancaster and York, until it was finally resolved by Henry Tudor's victory over Richard III at Bosworth.

The Tudor kings and queens who followed oversaw a period of relative stability at home despite religious turmoil in the wake of Henry VIII's break from Catholic Rome and his foundation of the protestant Church

FIG 6.1: Norham Castle was a major royal fortification along the Scottish border and had resisted numerous attacks and sieges over the centuries. In 1497 James IV of Scotland attacked Norham and brought with him a new weapon which the castle's medieval walls had not faced before, the cannon, including his prized piece of artillery, Mons Meg. Despite causing much damage the castle stood firm, but James was to try again 16 years later, this time with a mighty army and around 20 cannon. His destructive weapons allowed the outer ward to be overrun in a matter of days and they destroyed half of the great tower as shown here in this view. His success however was short-lived as the King and his army were defeated nearby at the Battle of Flodden on 9th September 1513.

FIG 6.2: Stokesay Castle, Shropshire: The castle still represented power and authority so when lesser nobles or ambitious gentry built a new home in the 14th and 15th century they imitated them and built curtain walls with battlements and towers surrounded by water-filled moats. These were not designed to withstand an attack, rather to make a statement for those families wishing to climb the social ladder. Even small manor houses and farmhouses could be set behind a moat which was more likely to be used for stocking fish than resisting an army. Stokesay Castle, pictured here, was begun in the late 1280s for a local wealthy wool merchant, Lawrence of Ludlow, who developed it not just as a fortified home but also as a valuable agricultural estate. With its large window openings and later timber framed additions it was in no position to resist a determined attack and during the English Civil War the garrison surrendered rather than face a siege.

Tournaments

Mock battles or a melee had been arranged by noblemen and kings from the 11th century as a type of sporting event to toughen up the nobility for war. They originally took the form of a battle in a open field with sometimes hundreds of knights and soldiers fighting within set rules, for instance whether weapons should be blunt or sharp (jousts became part of these events but were only a warming up exercise). They gave an opportunity for young nobles or the landless to catch the eye and climb the social ladder, for money to be made by ransoming captured knights, and for social contacts to be made and plots hatched. William Marshall, who became Regent of England in 1216 rose to fame by taking part in these 'tourneys' across Europe in his youth. However, they could become heated and violent and it was not unusual for some competitors to die. When the Earl of Pembroke was accidentally killed at a tournament in Hertford in 1241 the event disintegrated into a riot in which others lost their lives. Only the year before in Nuys, near Cologne, around 60 knights were recorded as being killed at another tournament. As a result the nobility began to change the way in which these events were held as they could ill afford to lose so many key men. Safety measures were taken to protect competitors and during the 14th century the more familiar medieval tournament evolved. The joust was now the main event with knights protected by plate armour, with lances which had hollow ends that shattered on impact, and a rail or fence between the charging horses called a tilt so they could not collide (hence the space where these were held is called a tilt yard). The tournament became a major social event controlled by rules of combat and the code of chivalry, with heralds identifying the coats of arms of competitors and extracting proper fees for entry.

The War of the Roses

Civil war broke out in 1455 for the right to rule England, between two parties; those who supported the existing but ineffective King Henry VI, the Lancastrians, and the Yorkists who fought for Richard, Duke of York, who was the wealthiest noble in the land and a claimant to the throne. The crown passed between both sides during thirty years of sporadic battles. The bloodiest of these was at Towton, Yorks in 1461 when the Yorkist forces now fighting for Edward, the son of Richard who had been killed the previous year outside Sandal Castle, routed the Lancastrians with records stating that over 25,000 died that day. In the aftermath, the Earl of Warwick, the Kingmaker, who was supporting Edward, laid siege to Bamburgh Castle in Northumberland which was belligerently held for the Lancastrians by Sir Ralph Grey. Warwick lined up a variety of artillery pieces and began bombarding the old walls causing much damage, with Grey knocked out by falling masonry in one such attack. With him out of the way the garrison quickly surrendered making this the first castle in England to fall to cannon and gunpowder.

FIG 6.3: Sandal Castle: This motte and bailey castle, with the site of the drawbridge and its pit in the foreground of this view, was the scene of a major battle during the War of the Roses. Richard Duke of York had captured King Henry VI but lacked the support to take the throne. Instead he had to quell the Lancastrians by force and headed north in December 1460 to Sandal Castle to confront them. Although he was outnumbered by the opposition in the valley below, for some unknown reason Richard sallied out from the castle on 30th December and attacked them only for his army to be massacred and the Yorkist claimant to the throne to be killed.

FIG 6.4: Baconsthorpe Castle, Norfolk: This fortified manor house was built in the 15th century, probably for the lawyer, John Heydon. Norfolk may have been far from the troublesome border regions but John had many enemies so he built these substantial towers and walls surrounded by a water-filled moat. Many of the so-called castles erected around this time were built in brick which was a fashionable sign of wealth rather than for making defensively strong walls.

of England. During the 16th century, attention turned from conquests abroad to defence of the realm, with the crown taking an active role in the building of coastal fortifications for the first time to keep foreign invaders at bay.

During this period the castle became more of a backdrop for a chivalric life, a prosperous estate and a romantic vision of Arthur and his Round Table rather than a garrisoned fortress. As the nobility of England began to feel reasonably secure in their position, their attention began to turn to making their home one which could impress guests with its grandeur and palatial accommodation. Their holdings would usually be more consolidated than in centuries before and they were no longer constantly travelling between them so now they could focus their time and effort on

FIG 6.5: Clifton Hall, Cumbria: Originally this was a modest manor house but as tensions rose along the Scottish border at the turn of the 16th century this fortified tower was built by William Wybergh to one side of it. These pele towers, as they are generally known, not only provided the family with a more defendable home but also made a statement about their social ambitions and Wybergh soon added additional accommodation to its southern face (you can see the stone corbels which supported its roof and the holes made for the floor joists in this view). Defence along the border would remain a concern even into the 18th century. The owner of Clifton Hall was abducted during the 1715 Jacobite rising and the hall was attacked and looted during the 1745 rebellion.

FIG 6.6: Lancaster Castle: This mighty gatehouse with machicolations and angled towers (rather than round) was built from the late 14th century as part of improvements to strengthen the royal castle after the city had been attacked and burnt by the Scots.

FIG 6.7: Dunvegan Castle, Isle of Skye: Most issues surrounding castles in Highland Scotland revolved around inter clan warfare which could lead to gruesome results. The MacLeods of Dunvegan were not only in conflict with the neighbouring MacDonald Clan for most of the 16th century but also had issues of inheritance within the clan itself. When the castle was captured in 1557 by Iain Dubh, who had attempted to make himself the legitimate heir by murdering the rightful son of the previous head, the Scottish regent ordered a force to be sent to recover Dunvegan. However, Iain's own clansmen had already forced him to flee to Harris and then Ireland where the O'Donnells murdered him by thrusting a red-hot iron into his bowels.

one or two key estates. The result was that many castles became neglected and fell into disuse; some became courtrooms and prisons while others which were personal favourites or conveniently located, could be lavished with major new domestic buildings. Grand halls with large stained glass windows and impressive timber roofs were erected within the castle walls and new private quarters were built close by as the nobility no longer wished to be mixed in with their household staff and garrison and sought private family space. Round towers, which were hard to undermine and could better resist the impact of a projectile were still fashionable but some reverted to square versions when building a new part of the castle as they provided a more convenient space inside at a time when defence was low on the list of priorities. Even the land around the fortifications could be converted to leisure with small gardens and paths laid out where once soldiers prepared for war while moats and lakes were created around the outer walls for show rather than to keep an army at bay. The castle was gradually transforming into a country residence and the only time many saw any military action was in the ever-popular tournaments which were held within their grounds.

Border castles

On the other hand, while most of England enjoyed a time of greater peace and stability there was still trouble in the border regions. Rebellions in Wales and a strong

Scottish Army able to raid into Northern England kept landowners in the areas close to these countries on edge. Existing castles remained active with many rebuilt, extended or fitted with improved defences during the 14th and 15th century. Lower down the social scale manor houses and farmsteads were fortified, not to resist an all-out attack from a major army but to be able to protect their assets from small-scale raiders. Tower houses were a popular form on both sides of the Scottish border, usually referred to as pele towers in England. These typically had three storeys with a parapet supported on corbels around the top and thick stone walls. A secure storage space was on the ground floor with steps on one side leading up to the main doorway and great hall on the first, from which access could be gained to the level below when the building was locked up at time of trouble. Throughout the 14th and 15th century new fortified houses were built until 1485 when Tudor Henry VII, who was of Welsh origin, came to the throne and in 1603 the union of the Scottish and English crowns under James I reduced the tensions along the borders.

Attacking castles in 14th to 16th century

The method of attacking and besieging castles did not fundamentally change during this period. Most clashes were on a smaller scale. Raids or rebellions lead by personal armies without the finance of the royal coffers; personal conflicts between two nobles arguing over ownership. Castles along the borders, and in Wales and Scotland were still taken by force, deception or by starving out the garrison.

Occasionally a larger force was used as part of an invasion, to try and extract a nobleman after a defeat in battle, or as part of a popular uprising. Some were driven by the religious turmoil of the 16th century. In 1536 a lawyer called Robert Aske, led the Pilgrimage of Grace, a revolt against Henry VIII's break with Rome and the Dissolution of the Monasteries, and attacked Scarborough Castle. Only 20 years later the castle was held by the supporters of Thomas Wyatt, who opposed the Catholicism of Queen Mary I.

However, during the 15th century a new weapon was being perfected which would change the way in which fortifications were built and would ultimately make medieval castles obsolete; the cannon. The first types which were used in Europe seem to have been vase-shaped weapons firing large arrows and were used by the English during the Hundred Years War against France. It was not until the 15th century the more familiar form of cannon with barrels forged

Iron hoops

Longitudinal iron bars

FIG 6.8: Mons Meg was one of the largest cannon from this period, made for the Duke of Burgundy in 1449, and then sent as a gift to King James II of Scotland. It had longitudinal iron bars strapped together by wrought iron hoops which were fused together to form the barrel (inset bottom left) which would have originally had a protective red coating. Mons Meg had a huge diameter of over 500mm (20 inches) which could fire large stone balls weighing around 175 kgs (385 lbs) and was used in sieges against the English. It currently stands in Edinburgh Castle.

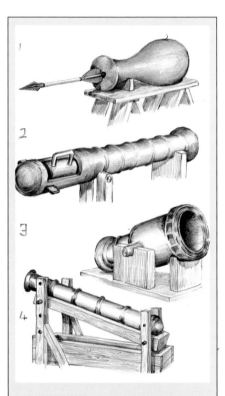

FIG 6.9. Artillery used during the 14th and 15th century varied in form and reliability, and were expensive pieces limited to the wealthiest nobles and royalty. The earliest to have been used in Europe were vase shaped pieces made from copper or brass which fired giant arrows or bolts (1). In the late 14th century iron began to be used for the barrels with some later types having a mug shaped cartridge (2) breach loaded (into the rear of the barrel). Bombards and mortars with large bores fired huge stone balls (3) and were used in siege warfare during the 15th century. Large cannon at this date were usually strapped onto fixed timber frames (4).

from strips of iron held together by metal bands were being used as siege weapons with ever larger 'bombards' given frightening names designed to strike fear into castle defenders. These early types were limited in a number of ways. They often needed a number of hours between firing and were also prone to exploding due to over use, or when the wrong measure of gunpowder was put in. King James II of Scotland, a keen advocate of modern artillery,

70

FIG 6.10: Warwick Castle: The barbican at this most entertaining of castles to visit can be seen here from above (left) projecting out from the front of the gatehouse. If any enemy managed to break through its gate they would then have to fight their way through the narrow passage (right) while arrows and bolts could be fired down from the flanking walls.

imported a number of cannon from Flanders as he tried to remove the English from Roxburgh Castle in 1460 but he was killed when one of them exploded during the siege. It was not until the late 15th century that new brass cannon from France, the use of cast iron balls rather than stone and improvements in the production of gunpowder made them a reliable and destructive weapon which could penetrate the walls of medieval fortifications.

Defending castles in 14th and 15th century

Although attention had turned towards improving the domestic arrangements in castles their defences were often improved with the latest features added even if these were more for show than effect. The gateway remained the weak point on most castles and further developments were made to protect it. From the late 13th century a pair of parallel walls was built out from the entrance of some castles to form a narrow passage, either in a straight line or with an angle, which led up to a new outer gate. This feature was called a barbican and it not only created yet another barrier for attackers to get through but also, if the enemy forced their way through

FIG 6.11: Gun loops: These appeared on British castles in the second half of the 14th century and became a common feature, especially in gatehouses, during the 15th. Early types usually had a round hole through the centre, some with an observation slit above making a keyhole shape. Later this vertical slit was often positioned away from the loop while those fitted by the turn of the 16th century had a square observation hole above a rectangular, splayed opening so the cannon had more room to be manoeuvred inside.

the first gate, they would have to pass along the narrow passage where they would have arrow fire and projectiles thrown down upon them from the tops of the flanking walls.

Just as the cannon was to become an effective weapon for attack so it could be equally devastating for defence. A stone or iron ball fired at close range could pass through a line of soldiers causing horrific injuries. Hence it became common in the 15th century for gun loops to be positioned either side of the gatehouse, covering the approach to the castle. It would take a brave man to run up to attack the entrance to a castle if they could see there were gun loops, although it is likely that many were fitted for the threat they posed alone without any

weapons actually being positioned behind them. Although cannon was an effective weapon, they were also expensive and were limited in number. The royal armouries could wield a wide range of weapons but many other castle owners may have only had a few portable cannon for show.

Coastal forts

During the Hundred Year War there were around 40 raids by French forces and pirates including numerous assaults upon the town of Rye and the port of Winchelsea. A number of wealthy families in the southern counties built their homes in the form of a castle with moats and curtain walls perhaps with this

72

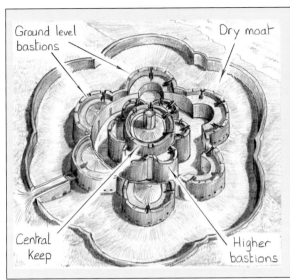

Ground level bastions

Dry moat

Central Keep

Higher bastions

FIG 6.12: Deal Castle, Kent: This 'device' fort built in 1539-40 was originally designed to house up to 140 guns, but at best had less than half that. Despite the expense and carefully planned design it did not see service in its first 100 years and had become neglected by the turn of the 17th century.

threat in mind. However, while the Kings of England still harboured ambitions to conquer France and spent vast sums of money and time pursuing this goal they made little effort to fortify defences along their own south coast. Traditionally, they had relied upon local lords to protect coastal regions and the Crown only built one castle during the 14th and 15th century at Queensborough, on the Isle of Sheppey. Queensborough was a cutting edge, circular planned, concentric castle, which along with work on the existing Hadleigh Castle in Essex was designed to protect the entrance to the Thames and Medway.

The final defeat of the English by the French not only dampened aspirations of empire building by the Crown but also focused royal minds upon Britain as an island nation, one which the Tudor Monarchs in the following century would make historic efforts to protect. With a new threat of invasion from France in the late 1530s, Henry VIII ordered the building of a chain of fortifications around the south coast from Essex in the east to Wales in the west. These Henrician castles or 'device' forts as they are known, initially had circular keeps and bastions arranged in steps so they could offer different ranges of fire. The problem with this was that in creating the tiered firing points the keep was too high and could have been an easy target for the enemy to hit. They also required a large number of guns and men to cover all parts of the fort due to its circular form and there were points close to the walls

73

FIG 6.13: Pendennis Castle, Cornwall: This fortification was completed for Henry VIII in 1542 to guard the mouth of the River Fal. In 1597 after a large Spanish fleet was only prevented from attacking the castle by bad weather, the Crown ordered a new ring of defences should be built around it, this time with earthworks to absorb cannonballs and new arrowhead bastions to give a better range of fire.

where adjoining points could not offer covering fire. A second series of forts incorporated new ideas from the continent and Yarmouth Castle on the Isle of Wight had a square plan with an arrowhead-shaped bastion to protect its landward side. This meant that fewer guns were required to cover all parts of the defences as the single bastion had a clear line of sight down both landward sides of the castle while the walls were made thick enough to absorb cannonballs.

These so-called castles however were strictly speaking forts. Despite still possessing the appearance of late medieval castles and being fitted with portcullis, drawbridges and moats, they were purely a military establishment and were not the home of a noble. For the Tudors, the castle was a thing of the past and their surveys of them in the mid-16th century found that most needed work and many were beyond worthwhile repair. Medieval castles were finished, or at least they thought so.

THE CASTLE REFORTIFIED
The English Civil War

Although the first Stuart King, James I, had joined the English and Scottish crowns he still had the legacy of religious divide between Catholics and Protestants, and issues with the monarchy and Parliament to contend with. James' character was such that these rarely boiled over during his reign but his son Charles I was not so politically talented. However, when he recalled Parliament in 1640 to raise money to suppress a Scottish rebellion few would believe that war was just around the corner. Even though he had alarmed his fiercely Protestant countrymen by taking a Catholic wife, and had exploited his royal powers by refusing to call a Parliament for nearly 12 years, the thought of taking up arms against the monarch and head of the Church of England was almost inconceivable. Yet only 18 months later the whole country would be involved in a destructive war, one in which castles, the outdated and crumbling relics of medieval warfare, would play a strategic part in gaining control of the country.

The English Civil War, fought between Charles' Royalist supporters and the Parliamentarians, initially ended when Charles was captured after four years of fighting, but continued sporadically as Royalist supporters raised armies and caused rebellions which were not finally crushed by the Parliamentarians until the Battle of Worcester in 1651. Unlike early medieval warfare which was centred around the castle, the English Civil War was decided on the open battlefield with musketeers and pikemen flanked by cavalry forming opposing forces which could destroy each other in a matter of hours. Many medieval castles provided both armies and their supporters with a base from which to carry out raids and a last bastion to fall back to after defeat in the field. As most had become ruined or at least poorly maintained they were usually refortified, some with the latest style earthwork defences and positions for cannon erected around their ancient walls. Even fortified manor houses and similar residences would provide some belligerent nobles with a defensive shelter from inevitable capture, a role their mock battlements and decorative towers were never intended to face.

FIG 7.1: Scarborough Castle: There had been a fortification upon this promontory high above the harbour at Scarborough since at least Roman times. However, the Parliamentarians considered the castle held for the King as a nuisance rather than a priority. This allowed its commander to raid the surrounding countryside, safely land arms for the Royalist army and use the harbour from which to attack ships bringing vital coal supplies down from Newcastle to London. It would not be until March 1645 that the Parliamentarians under Sir John Meldrum finally laid siege to the castle into which the Royalist commander Sir Hugh Cholmley had retreated with time for him to establish new defences and store supplies. Meldrum brought up the largest cannon in the country at the time, The Cannon Royal, in the church just below the castle gatehouse and proceeded to pound the castle taking down part of the keep (the soldiers in this view are firing out of its ruins) while Chomley's force fired back destroying much of the church. The rubble provided the defenders with shelter from which to fire and the siege continued to ebb and flow through the Spring with almost continuous firing, making this one of the bloodiest of all sieges. Finally, at the end of July, after Meldrum had been mortally wounded, the new Parliamentarian commander began a bombardment from land and sea that forced the garrison, running low on supplies and riddled with disease, to finally surrender.

Castles during the English Civil War

As soon as the descent towards conflict became inevitable many old deserted castles, and those which had become purely domestic accommodation had their defences re-established or bolstered with arms and supplies sourced so the men stationed there could hope to last out a siege. The Tower of London, which contained much of the Crown's wealth at the start of the war, was secured for the King with new gun positions built and a garrison of London's Trained Bands installed. These were local militia established by Queen Elizabeth I with membership compulsory for those who held land and property, although they would often send their servants to training sessions in their place. Trained bands were

FIG 7.2: Arundel Castle, Sussex: The Howard family home was garrisoned with around 800 Royalist soldiers during the war. With such a force the Parliamentarians lacked the manpower to take the castle after they had seized the town and they instead laid siege to it. Their commander William Waller had the lake below it drained, cutting off their water supply and then forced the garrison's surrender in January 1644 after he brought in new, larger cannon. The castle was partly demolished (slighted) after the war but unlike many others it was gradually restored by the Howard family during the 18th and 19th century to form the glorious home we see today.

the only permanent army in the country at the time and the regiments from London were well trained. However, those in the Tower switched sides in 1642 and allowed Parliament to install its own commander, so for the duration of the war the Tower remained securely in their hands.

Henry Hastings, a Royalist officer in the Midlands, prepared his old family castle in Ashby de la Zouch for war by pulling down buildings in the surrounding area to clear space and to provide materials to

FIG 7.3: Newark Castle, Notts: Despite having a less than formidable façade punctuated by windows, Newark Castle and the town defences were never breached during a number of sieges in the war. It only surrendered on the orders of the King after he had handed himself over to the parliamentary forces in 1646.

refortify it, as well as creating new defensive positions. As it turned out the castle was surrendered at the end of the conflict rather than becoming besieged. At Warwick Castle, walls were heightened, gun positions built from timbers and soil and gunpowder sourced for their cannon. Despite the importance of cannon there were only limited numbers available, so when the castle was attacked in August 1642 by a Royalist force they could only pound the walls with two small guns which are recorded as having little effect on the medieval fortress other than to frighten those inside.

As war spread, London, most major cities and much of the east and south of the country sided with the Parliamentarians while the King found most support in the north and west of Britain. Corfe Castle, Dorset which Charles's Attorney General had left in the hands of his wife, Lady Mary Banks, with a handful of armed men, quickly found itself surrounded by enemy forces. After a plan to covertly break in during a hunt in May 1643 failed, the parliamentary forces decided to besiege the castle with over 500 men, although their delay had allowed Lady Banks time to call supplies in and bolster her garrison to around 80. She successfully held out for over six weeks, suffering hardly any casualties while the besiegers lost over one hundred and were then forced into retreat when a Royalist force relieved the castle. Corfe finally fell towards the end of the war when one of Lady Banks' officers betrayed them. After leaving the castle during a new siege to bring back Royalist reinforcements he actually returned with Parliamentarians in disguise who overwhelmed the garrison inside to coincide with an attack launched by the besiegers.

Unlike those castles which were still occupied at the outbreak of war there were others in ruins which were brought back into service. Beeston Castle, on an outcrop of rock high above the Cheshire plain was taken by the Parliamentarians in February 1643 and its old walls repaired and defences cleaned out. One night in December that year a Royalist captain and eight of his men managed to get inside the fortress and surprise its commander, Captain Steele, who was later shot for his failure to hold onto the castle. The Royalists clung onto Beeston throughout a siege lasting most of 1645 and only surrendered when their food ran out.

By 1644 the war was turning against the Royalists. At Lincoln, Oliver Cromwell commanded the siege of the castle at the same time as holding off a relieving Royalist force. Despite the importance of cannon this castle was taken using old-style methods. Cromwell's forces crept up at night with ladders to scale the walls while the Royalist defenders threw boulders down upon them until some of his men managed to get onto the ramparts and then force the garrison's surrender. At Montgomery in Powys, close to the English border, the Royalist castle on a hill above the town fell to the Parliamentarians in September 1644. However, they were taken by surprise a few days later when a Royalist force laid siege to the castle and split the Parliamentary forces. Around 500 retreated into the castle while the cavalry rode off to get help. The relieving force arrived a week later and in the ensuing battle to the north of the town they routed the Royalist force while the Parliamentarians in the castle sallied out and defeated those who had stayed behind to maintain the siege.

After the defeat of the Royalist army at the Battle of Naseby in June 1645 many of their supporters retreated to their castles and estates. It would take nearly a year before the Parliamentarians were able to crush

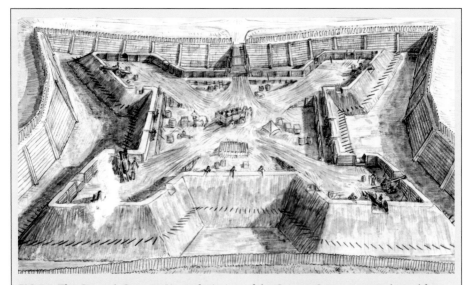

FIG 7.4: The Queen's Sconce, Newark: A view of the Queens Sconce, a star-shaped fort, as it may have appeared during the Civil War. In this period defences built for cannon featured distinctive arrow head bastions, a form which had been imported from the continent and were first installed at coastal forts in the late 16th century. They allowed cannon and muskets to not only fire out from a safe position behind deep earthworks which could absorb enemy fire, but also to cover all parts of the defences should the enemy get into the dry moat. The earthworks, which are still clearly visible on the ground today to the south of Newark, were part of the town's defences which kept the Parliamentarians at bay for the duration of the war.

these remaining outposts held for the King. The Parliamentary commanders Thomas Fairfax and Oliver Cromwell then took their army to the south west and established control of a number of towns before surrounding Nunney Castle, Somerset in September 1645. Unwisely Richard Prater, who owned the impressive moated site, refused to surrender and even waved a flag with a catholic crucifix above the walls to taunt the besiegers. It only took a few days for Fairfax's and Cromwell's cannon to breach the castle's walls and render it useless so that Prater had to surrender and also promise to support Parliament and never to return to his castle.

Newark Castle and its market town were strategically important as they stood alongside the River Trent at the junction between the Great North Road and Fosse Way. Defensive earthworks and forts had been dug around the town and it had already endured two sieges during the war. Now in the wake of the defeat at Naseby, the Royalist garrison and townsfolk soon found themselves surrounded by a huge Scottish Army to the north and a Parliamentarian one to the south. Siege works were established and the local river which served the grain mills was dammed up as they tried to starve out the town but despite having to resort to eating horses and dogs the Royalists held out throughout winter and only surrendered in May 1646 after the King had handed himself over to the Scots and to Parliament.

Despite this action there were still a few troublesome outposts of Royalist support. At Goodrich Castle, Herefordshire, Sir Henry Lingen had been carrying out raids on parliamentary forces from his secure base and even after his horses had

FIG 7.5: Roaring Meg, Goodrich Castle, Herefordshire: A mortar was a stubby, light cannon designed to send explosive shells in a high trajectory over a short distance. They were first used for siege work in the late 15th century but Roaring Meg, cast in a foundry close to Goodrich Castle, was the largest so far in England. Unlike most cannon at the time which shot solid balls Roaring Meg could fire round metal shells filled with gunpowder, weighing up to 90kg (200lbs), which would explode on impact (an example which failed to ignite is on show in the castle).

been captured and stables destroyed in a surprise attack, the Royalists were still able to cause trouble. With this in mind the Roundheads, under Colonel John Birch, returned in June 1646 to besiege the castle but found that the medieval structure was too strong to attack directly. Earthworks were dug for artillery, a new mortar cannon was cast specifically for the siege, and miners and sappers were brought into undermine the north west tower. The garrison inside soon realised that Birch's men were mining towards the tower and started digging their own tunnel to intercept it but before they could reach it Birch used his mortar Roaring Meg at close range and finally brought the structure down, which also collapsed the Royalist counter mine. With the defences breached, Lingen and its garrison surrendered on 31st July.

Slighting

Castles had helped to prolong the conflict by providing a last-ditch defence for Royalist supporters and had become a point from which they could launch raids. It was clear to Parliamentarian leaders that they could also provide bases for any future uprising in support of the King, as happened in 1648 and again a few years later. Hence it was decided that their military threat would need to be neutralised. Some were so badly damaged by artillery

attacks that they were deemed to pose no threat. Sometimes the local population were keen to be rid of a castle as at Pontefract, where the townsfolk who had endured three sieges through the conflict supported its destruction as they felt it had been a magnet for trouble. Others were saved because the local population petitioned Parliament so it could be retained for local use, usually as a court or prison.

However, many medieval castles were strategically well placed, with effective defences and durable walls so that there was no other course for the Parliamentarians than to render them unusable. This 'slighting' usually involved the destruction of a section of the keep or a crucial part of the defences so that it would be impossible to effectively defend them in future. Gunpowder was often used to achieve this with barrels placed under walls which were sent crashing down never to be rebuilt again. This was a quick and effective method of removing their threat especially as a complete demolition was often impractical or would have been expensive and time-consuming. The dramatic form many ruined castles present today, with their staggered walls and cracked buildings, is often due to this post-Civil War slighting. After the restoration of the monarchy in 1660 many castles were returned to their former owners. Some left the old fortifications to ruin and built a new fashionable, Classical style house nearby. Others restored the domestic parts and lived in them for a while although they had often moved out and their castle had often been downgraded to a farmhouse by the early 18th century. In some cases, they were purchased by opportunists who stripped the castle of its valuable materials like lead and sold off the masonry and timber for other building projects. It would not be until the early 19th century that a wave a national patriotism during the Napoleonic Wars and the creation of literature which romanticised the medieval period that castles became fashionable again. The Victorians' passion for the Gothic inspired many wealthy landowners to restore old ruins while the creation of national societies to protect these ancient remains began to reverse the centuries of neglect and save this rich legacy of British medieval military architecture for future generations.

FIG 7.6: Carlisle Castle: This major English castle close to the border with Scotland has become the most besieged castle in Britain and was one of the last medieval castles to see military action. During the Jacobite Rising of 1745 Bonnie Prince Charlie's forces, which had invaded England in November that year, surrounded Carlisle and after a brief siege the frightened population surrendered and the Jacobites took possession of the castle and its store of arms. Although the fear created by the fall of the English city and its castle created panic further south, Bonnie Prince Charlie's forces stalled at Derby and his indecisive generals convinced him to retreat during which he left a force of 400 to hold Carlisle. The advancing British under the command of the Duke of Cumberland laid siege to Carlisle Castle and battered its western wall with cannon until it was breached and they were able to retake the castle on 30th December 1745.

PLACES TO VISIT

Britain is blessed with a large and rich heritage of medieval castles. There are over a thousand sites and many hundreds of these have standing remains and are open to the public. The following websites are very useful for finding where they are and discovering more about them:

www.castlesfortsbattles.co.uk
www.castleuk.net
www.castlexplorer.co.uk
www.gatehouse-gazetteer.info
www.historic-uk.com/HistoryMagazine/DestinationsUK/CastlesinEngland/
en.wikipedia.org/wiki/List_of_castles_in_England

Many of the finest medieval castles are maintained in England by **English Heritage**, in Wales by **Cadw** (the Welsh word meaning 'to keep or protect') and in Scotland by **Historic Scotland**. Some castles in their care are free to enter at any reasonable hour, others have a charge, although if you are planning to visit a number of sites then explorer passes or annual membership are excellent value. The **National Trust** and **National Trust for Scotland** also have a number of outstanding castles in their care. Many of these have been later rebuilt as country residences but they still retain many of their defensive features. For more information on access, opening times, prices and dates of special events and re-enactments check the following websites:

www.english-heritage.org.uk
www.cadw.gov.wales
www.historicenvironment.scot
www.nationaltrust.org.uk
www.nts.org.uk

The list below includes the castles which feature in this book along with some other notable sites and personal favourites. They are all open to the public with many of them having access most of the year. Others have more restricted times which can be checked on the websites listed.

SOUTHERN ENGLAND

Arundel Castle, Arundel, West Sussex, BN18 9AB. ☎ 01903 882173.
⊕ www.arundelcastle.org. *An early Norman castle with its original motte and keep surrounded by later buildings.*
Carisbrooke Castle, Castle Hill, Newport, Isle of Wight, PO30 1XY.
☎ 01983 522107. ⊕ www.english-heritage.org.uk/visit/places/carisbrooke-castle. *Impressive castle with an early stone keep which was besieged by the French and used to imprison Charles I after the English Civil War, prior to his execution.*
Corfe Castle, The Square, Corfe Castle, Wareham, Dorset, BH20 5EZ.
☎ 01929 481294. ⊕ www.nationaltrust.org.uk/corfe-castle. *Dramatic ruins of this once mighty castle set in beautiful countryside. Earthworks of a siege castle can be seen on satellite mapping 400m south west of the castle.*
Deal Castle, Marine Road, Walmer, Deal, Kent, CT14 7BA. ☎ 01304 372762.
⊕ www.english-heritage.org.uk/visit/places/deal-castle. *One of the earliest Tudor coastal forts which is largely in its original form.*
Dover Castle, Castle Hill, Dover, Kent, CT16 1HU. ☎ 01304 211 067.
⊕ www.english-heritage.org.uk/visit/places/dover-castle. *One of Britain's major castles which has been an important military fortification for over 800 years. Not only is there the castle and its impressive keep, towers and gatehouse but also a Roman lighthouse, Saxon church and underground tunnels.*
Nunney Castle, Castle Street, Nunney, Frome, Somerset, BA11 4LW.
⊕ www.english-heritage.org.uk/visit/places/nunney-castle. *An attractive 14th-century tower with a moat which was slighted after a siege during the English Civil War.*
Pendennis Castle, Falmouth, Cornwall, TR11 4LP, ☎ 01326 316594.
⊕ www.english-heritage.org.uk/visit/places/pendennis-castle. *A Tudor artillery fortress set within later earthworks with arrowhead bastions. St Mawes Castle, an excellently preserved Henrician fort, is only a mile away across the estuary.*
Pevensey Castle, Castle Road, Pevensey, East Sussex, BN24 5LE. ☎ 01323 762604.
⊕ www.english-heritage.org.uk/visit/places/pevensey-castle. *The site of the first castle erected by William the Conqueror when he landed in 1066. The remains include walls from the earlier Roman fort and a later 13th-century curtain walled castle.*
Restormel Castle, Lostwithiel, Cornwall, PL22 0EE, ☎ 01208 872687.
⊕ www.english-heritage.org.uk/visit/places/restormel-castle. *One of the best examples of a shell keep set upon an Norman motte.*
Rochester Castle, Rochester, Kent, ME1 1SW. ☎ 01634 335882.
⊕ www.english-heritage.org.uk/visit/places/rochester-castle. *Impressive Norman stone keep with one round tower which replaced the original after it was destroyed in the siege of 1215.*
Tower of London, London, EC3N 4AB. ☎ 020 3166 6000.
⊕ www.hrp.org.uk/tower-of-london. *This famous landmark with the Norman keep, after which it is named, is at the centre of a series of defences which show many aspects of military development over the centuries.*

Windsor Castle, Windsor, Berks, SL4 1NJ. ☎ 0303 123 7304.
⊕ www.royalcollection.org.uk/visit/windsorcastle. *This glorious fortification high above the River Thames is the oldest and largest occupied castle in the world.*

CENTRAL ENGLAND
Beeston Castle, Chapel Lane, Beeston, Cheshire, CW6 9TX. ☎ 01829 260464.
⊕ www.english-heritage.org.uk/visit/places/beeston-castle-and-woodland-park. *There are the remains of the 13th-century gatehouse and spectacular views, which make the walk up this hill on the Cheshire plain worthwhile.*
Bolsover Castle, Castle Street, Bolsover, Derbyshire, S44 6PR. ☎ 01246 822844.
⊕ www.english-heritage.org.uk/visit/places/bolsover-castle. *The original Norman castle was rebuilt as a Stuart mansion in the early 17th century by William Cavendish before he went into exile during the Civil War.*
Bridgnorth Castle, Castle St, Bridgnorth, Shropshire, WV16 4AF. ☎ 07500 937092.
The remains of the keep at one end of this attractive hilltop town are leaning over after it was blown up following the English Civil War.
Castle Rising Castle, Castle Rising, Kings Lynn, Norfolk, PE31 6AH.
[☎] 01553 631330. ⊕ www.english-heritage.org.uk/visit/places/castle-rising-castle. *Well preserved Norman keep set within impressive earthworks.*
Clun Castle, Clun, Craven Arms, Shropshire, SY7 8JT. ⊕ www.english-heritage. org.uk/visit/places/clun-castle. *Excellent condition motte and bailey earthworks with remains of large stone keep to one side.*
Framlingham Castle, Church Street, Framlingham, Suffolk, IP13 9BP.
☎ 01728 724922. ⊕ www.english-heritage.org.uk/visit/places/framlingham-castle. *A rare early curtain walled castle which has been extensively restored so you can walk around a large part of its ramparts.*
Goodrich Castle, Castle Lane, Goodrich, Ross on Wye, Herefordshire, HR9 6HY.
☎ 01600 890538. ⊕ www.english-heritage.org.uk/visit/places/goodrich-castle. *Mighty castle remains with Roaring Meg, the only surviving English Civil War mortar.*
Kenilworth Castle, Castle Green, Kenilworth, Warwickshire, CV8 1NG.
[☎] 01926 852078. [⊕] www.english-heritage.org.uk/visit/places/kenilworth-castle. *A major medieval castle which influenced the design of many late 13th-century fortifications after its defences managed to keep out the might of the royal army during the siege in 1266. Also features a mighty keep, great hall, and Elizabethan garden and gatehouse.*
Kirby Muxloe Castle, Oakcroft Ave, Kirby Muxloe, Leicestershire, LE9 2DH.
☎ 01162 386886. ⊕ www.english-heritage.org.uk/visit/places/kirby-muxloe-castle. *An attractive 15th-century red brick fortified manor house surrounded by a water-filled moat, built for Lord Hastings who was executed by Richard III before it was completed.*
Lincoln Castle, Castle Hill, Lincoln, LN1 3AA. ☎ 01522 554559.
⊕ www.lincolncastle.com. *Major castle opposite the cathedral which now has a walk*

around the complete circumference of its walls and a Victorian prison.
Ludlow Castle, Castle Square, Ludlow, Shropshire, SY8 1AY. ☎ 01584 873355.
⊕ www.ludlowcastle.com. *Impressive castle with keep, tower and walls as well as a rare circular chapel.*
Newark Castle, Castlegate, Newark, Nottinghamshire, NG24 1BG. ☎ 01636 655765.
The shell of the west front of the castle overlooks the River Trent. The Queens Sconce, NG24 4AU, a rare English Civil War earthwork fort, is three quarters of a mile to the south west of the castle.
Norwich Castle, Castle Meadow, Norwich, NR1 3JU. ☎ 01603 493625.
⊕ www.museums.norfolk.gov.uk/norwich-castle. *Massive Norman keep built on top of the earlier motte which was later converted into a prison. Excellent exhibits and tours around the buildings.*
Stokesay Castle, Stokesay, Craven Arms, Shropshire, SY7 9AH. ☎ 01588 672544.
⊕ www.english-heritage.org.uk/visit/places/stokesay-castle. *Rustic fortified manor house with great hall, tower and distinctive timber-framed gatehouse.*
Warwick Castle, Warwick, CV34 4QU.
☎ 0871 265 2000.
⊕ www.warwick-castle.com. *One of the most exciting castles to visit, not only with walks around its walls and towers but also has the world's largest working trebuchet.*

Warwick Castle

NORTHERN ENGLAND
Bamburgh Castle, Bamburgh, Northumberland , NE69 7DF. ☎ 01668 214515.
⊕ www.bamburghcastle.com. *Iconic castle set on an outcrop of rock above the Northumberland coast with a fascinating history, including a number of notable sieges.*
Brougham Castle, Moor Lane, Penrith, Cumbria, CA10 2AA. ☎ 01768 862488.
⊕ www.english-heritage.org.uk/visit/places/brougham-castle. *This formidable 13th-century castle beside the River Eamont was built with Scottish invasions in mind.*
Carlisle Castle, Castle Way, Carlisle, Cumbria, CA3 8UR. ☎ 01228 591922.
⊕ www.english-heritage.org.uk/visit/places/carlisle-castle. *This vital border castle has been the subject of more sieges than any other in Britain. The impressive site includes sandstone walls, keep, towers and gatehouse as well as the earthworks of a Tudor artillery battery.*

Clifford's Tower, Tower Street, York, North Yorkshire, YO1 9SA. ☎ 01904 646940: ⊕ www.english-heritage.org.uk/visit/places/cliffords-tower-york. *A 13th-century shell keep built on top of the original castle motte after the original timber keep had been burnt down during the mass suicide and massacre of the city's Jewish community in 1190.*

Conisbrough Castle, Castle Hill, Conisbrough, Doncaster, South Yorkshire, DN12 3BU. ☎ 01709 863329. ⊕ www.english-heritage.org.uk/visit/places/ conisbrough-castle. *Rare cylindrical keep with prominent buttresses which dominates the bailey of this important castle.*

Dunstanburgh Castle, Dunstanburgh Road, Craster, Alnwick, Northumberland, NE66 3TT. ☎ 01665 576231. Websites: http://www.english-heritage.org.uk/visit/ places/dunstanburgh-castle or www.nationaltrust.org.uk/dunstanburgh-castle. *This huge castle is dominated by the great gatehouse and was originally surrounded by large lakes probably to impress visitors rather than make it impregnable. It is just down the coast from Bamburgh and is owned by the National Trust and managed by English Heritage.*

Lancaster Castle, Castle Parade, Lancaster, LA1 1YJ. ☎ 01524 64998. ⊕ www.lancastercastle.com. *An important military position used by the Romans on which now stands the medieval castle with its imposing 14th-century gatehouse. Daily tours include the later prison which forms a large part of the site.*

Newcastle Castle, The Black Gate, Castle Garth, Newcastle Upon Tyne, NE1 1RQ. ☎ 0191 230 6300. ⊕ www.newcastlecastle.co.uk. *The gatehouse and keep survive from this castle conveniently positioned close to the city centre and its landmark buildings, bridges and famous Grey Street.*

Norham Castle, Castle Street, Norham, Northumberland, TD15 2JY. ⊕ www.english-heritage.org.uk/visit/places/norham-castle. *An important border castle overlooking the River Tweed which was besieged numerous times. The last one, using cannon, resulted in the destruction of much of its walls and keep.*

Richmond Castle, Tower Street, Richmond, Yorks, DL10 4QW. ☎ 01748 822493. ⊕ www.english-heritage.org.uk/visit/places/richmond-castle. *This attractive market town is dominated by the medieval keep which doubled up as the gatehouse for the castle.*

Sandal Castle, Manygates Lane, Sandal, Wakefield, Yorks, WF2 7DS. ☎ 01927 249779. ⊕ www.wakefield.gov.uk/events-and-culture/castles/sandal-castle. *Well preserved motte and bailey castle with views across the valley where the Battle of Wakefield took place in 1460.*

Scarborough Castle, Castle Road, Scarborough, Yorks, YO11 1HY. ☎ 01723 372451. ⊕ www.english-heritage.org.uk/visit/places/scarborough-castle. *The remains of the walls, barbican and keep, which was partially destroyed during the siege in the English Civil War, stand on top of this promontory along with the remains of a Roman signal station.*

SCOTLAND

Caerlaverock Castle, Glencaple, Dumfries, DG1 4RU. ☎ 01387 770 244.
⊕ www.historicenvironment.scot/visit-a-place/places/caerlaverock-castle. *Beautiful triangular-shaped castle reflected in its water-filled moat. There is a fascinating gatehouse, a stunning 17th-century lodge with carved gables and endless passages and rooms to explore.*
Drumcoltran Tower, Kirkgunzeon, Dumfries and Galloway, DG2 8LF. ⊕ www.historicenvironment.scot/visit-a-place/places/drumcoltran-tower. *A well preserved Tower House.*
Dunnottar Castle, Stonehaven, AB39 2TL. ☎ 01569 762173. ⊕ www.dunnottarcastle. co.uk. *Dramatic castle set high above the cliffs with a range of buildings from various dates on this ancient fortified site.*
Dunvegan Castle, Dunvegan, Isle of Skye, IV55 8WF. ☎ 01470 521206.

Caerlaverock Castle

⊕ www.dunvegancastle.com. *A beautifully positioned castle which has been the home of the Clan MacLeod for over 800 years, making it the oldest continuously inhabited castle in Scotland.*
Edinburgh Castle, The Esplanade, Edinburgh, EH1 2NG. ☎ 0131 225 9846.
⊕ www.historicenvironment.scot/visit-a-place/places/edinburgh-castle. *This iconic castle dominating the rocky outcrop high above the city is rightly very popular and highly rated and includes the Mons Meg cannon along its ramparts.*
Motte of Urr, Haugh of Urr, Dumfries and Galloway, DG7 3JZ. *The well preserved remains of a motte and bailey castle. Access from a parking space along B794 about 2 miles north of Dalbeattie, then cross the bridge over the Urr Water to reach the castle.*
Stirling Castle, Castle Wynd, Old Town, Stirling, FK8 1EJ. ☎ ☎ 01786 450 000.
⊕ www.historicenvironment.scot/visit-a-place/places/stirling-castle. *An important castle and royal palace for the Scottish monarchy with its impressive buildings high above the site of battles and sieges.*

WALES

Beaumaris Castle, Beaumaris, Isle of Anglesey, LL58 8AP. ☎ 01248 810361.
⊕ cadw.gov.wales/daysout/beaumaris-castle. *Don't be fooled by its rustic appearance reflected in the moat; this was a militarily advanced medieval castle with concentric walls and is of international importance, even though it was never fully completed to its original plans.*
Caernarfon Castle, Caernarfon, LL55 2AY. ☎ 01286 677617.
⊕ cadw.gov.wales/daysout/caernarfon-castle. *Monumental walls and towers surround this historically important castle.*

Caerphilly Castle, Caerphilly, CF83 1JD.
☎ 029 2088 3143. ⊕ cadw.gov.wales/
daysout/caerphilly-castle. *One of the finest
castles to visit in Britain not only because
of its historic importance and impressive
concentric design but also because it has
replica siege engines and hoarding, and
some fantastic dragons.*
Castell y bere, north of Abergynolwyn, nr
Tywyn, LL36 9TP. ☎ 02920 500200.
⊕ cadw.gov.wales/daysout/castell-y-bere.

Caerphilly Castle

*A native Welsh castle set in a beautiful, remote valley north east of Tywyn, which was
built, besieged and abandoned all in the 13th century.*
Coity Castle, West Plas Road, Bridgend, CF35 6BG. ☎ 01443 336000.
⊕ cadw.gov.wales/daysout/coitycastle. *An attractive castle with the remains of the
curtain wall, keep, gatehouse and moat dating from the late 12th to 14th century,
which was strong enough to resist sieges during the Welsh rebellion in the early
15th century.*
Conwy Castle, Conwy, LL32 8AY. ☎ 01492 592358. ⊕ cadw.gov.wales/daysout/
conwycastle. *Another impressive castle built by Edward along a ridge above the
River Conwy estuary. The twin wards surrounded by curtain walls and towers are
complemented by the medieval walled town which was built alongside.*
Dryslwyn Castle, B4297, Carmarthen, SA32 8JQ. ⊕ cadw.gov.wales/daysout/
dryslwyncastle. *The crumbling ruins set high on a hill overlooking the Tywi valley are
all that remain of the castle which had three wards and a small town, all devastated by
a siege in 1287.*
Flint Castle, Flint, CH6 5PF. ⊕ cadw.gov.wales/daysout/flintcastle. *A unique stone
castle beside the Dee estuary with curtain walls featuring an isolated round keep
which was defendable in its own right should the rest of the castle be overrun.*
Harlech Castle, Harlech, LL46 2YH. ☎ 01766 780 552. ⊕ cadw.gov.wales/daysout/
harlechcastle. *One of Edward I's most impressive castles with concentric walls, towers
and powerful gatehouses positioned on a rocky outcrop high above Cardigan Bay.*
Rhuddlan Castle, Rhuddlan, LL18 5AD. ☎ 01745 590777.
⊕ cadw.gov.wales/daysout/rhuddlancastle. *Another of Edward I's new castles built
with the latest 13th-century features and positioned with direct access to the River
Clwyd which he had dredged so ships could bring supplies in.*

Glossary

Allure: Another name for the wall walk which runs behind the battlements.

Arrow loop: Vertical slit in a wall or merlon for archers to fire through. A horizontal part could be added for crossbowmen. A triangular base increased the field of fire along the base of the walls.

Bailey: The enclosed space originally attached to a motte in which the garrison were accommodated and stores held. As castles were rebuilt in stone so the enclosures created within new curtain walls were sometimes called baileys or wards.

Ballista: A large crossbow which was mounted on a base and could fire a long bolt with enough power to pass through a number of men. Although it could be used by attackers it was more useful for defenders.

Barbican: An extension to the gateway with a pair of flanking walls and an outer gateway which allowed defenders to fire down upon attackers in a tight narrow space before they even reached the main entrance.

Bartizan: A small turret projecting from the top corner of a tower or gatehouse.

Bastion: A projection from a wall or earthworks upon which armed men or artillery could be mounted.

Battlements: The parapet along the top of a wall or tower with regularly spaced openings (merlons and crenels). Also known as crenellations.

Belfry: Another name for a siege tower.

Berm: Flat strip of land between a ditch and bank, or in a castle between the moat and walls.

Brattice: Temporary, covered wooden platforms built out from a wall or tower for defenders to drop missiles or fire down upon attackers at the base of a wall. More commonly called hoarding.

Buttress: A projecting vertical masonry or brick strip along the outside of a wall to help support it or transfer the thrust from the roof of buildings.

Concentric walls: A ring of tall masonry wall within a lower ring so that archers could fire from the inner over the top of the outer.

Constable/Castellan: The official who took charge of the castle in his master's absence.

Corbel: A stone bracket projecting out from a wall which usually supported timber floor and roof joists or machicolations.

Crenel: The open section of the battlements. Also known as embrasures.

Crenellations: Another word for the battlements

Cross wall: A dividing wall within the keep. It could support the roof and floors as well as act as an internal barrier to attackers.

Curtain walls: The short lengths of wall which appeared to hang between towers (hence curtain). Today it is usually used to refer to any type of stone or brick wall around a castle.

Donjon: Another word for the keep.

Drawbridge: A flat wooden bridge in front of a gateway which could be lifted or hinged up against the face of the gate opening a gap over the moat.

referred to as a pont levis/raised bridge.

Dungeon: An underground chamber used for prisoners. Derived from the word donjon.

Embrasure: Another word for crenel.

Forebuilding: An extension in front of the entrance to a keep which usually housed the steps up to the door and a number of additional chambers.

Garderobe: A medieval toilet, usually found at the end of a short angled passage within the thickness of the walls.

Gun loop: A round hole or horizontal opening (sometimes with a vertical sighting slit) used for cannon to fire out at attackers. Usually found in the gatehouse.

Herrisons: Lines of pointed stakes bound together in an open scissor form (from the French for hedgehog).

Hoarding: Temporary, covered wooden platforms built out from a wall or tower for defenders to drop missiles or fire down upon attackers at the base of a wall. Also known as a brattice.

Keep: The name, commonly used from the 16th century, for the great tower or donjon. This was the main building within a castle or on top of a motte which provided accommodation for the owner and a point where he and his followers could retreat to.

Machicolations: A permanent, shorter, stone version of hoarding or bratticing supported on corbels with slots through which missiles could be dropped on attackers.

Mangonel: A torsion powered large catapult which had an arm set in a twisted material which sprung up when released hurling a projectile from the

cup or sling at its end towards the target.

Merlon: The solid part of the battlements which stood between the crenels.

Moat: A wide defensive ditch dug around the walls of a castle which could be either dry or filled with water (especially on later castles).

Motte: The large mound upon which was originally placed a timber keep or tower, with the bailey attached to one side below (hence motte and bailey castle).

Mural: Relating to a wall. It is applied in castles to passages in the thickness of the walls or to towers placed in the line of a wall.

Murder holes/meurtrières: Gaps in the ceiling of an entrance passage through which defenders could drop missiles or hot sand but which were more likely to have been used for water to put out fires set against the wooden gates.

Oubliette: A bottle shaped underground chamber with a trap door at the top which was used as a dungeon.

Palisade: A defensive wall usually on top of a bank made from vertical timbers or posts.

Pele tower: A stone or occasionally timber tower usually of three or four storeys, either set within an enclosure or attached to a large house, which was used as a defendable home for a wealthy farmer or landowner. Most date from the 14th and 15th century and are found in the North of England.

Pentise/Penthouse/Sow: A movable shelter with a sloping or double pitched cover which was used to protect attackers who were undermining the castle walls or operating a battering ram from missiles and arrows fired down by the defenders.

Perrier: A stone throwing, counterweighted siege engine which had a pivoted arm with one end pulled by a group of men or women so that the other holding the projectile would swing round and hurl it towards the target.

Portcullis: A wood and iron grid that could be lowered down on chains in front or behind a gate. From the Old French porte coleice, meaning sliding gate.

Postern gate: A small gate or doorway set in the outer walls which could be used as an escape route or for the defenders to sally out and attack the besiegers. Also known as a sally port.

Putlog hole: A small socket in a wall which was used to support timber scaffolding during construction.

Quoins: The stones which form the outer corners of a building.

Revetting: A stone or timber facing of an earth bank or sides of a ditch which were used to hold the soil in place and protect it from weathering. Some castle

mottes and the steep sides of dry ditches may have been treated in this way.

Rubble: Rough, random sized stones set in mortar which formed the core of most castle walls.

Sally port: A small gate or doorway set in the outer walls which could be used for defenders to sally out and attack the besiegers. Also known as a postern gate.

Slighting: To damage a castle in such a way as to render it undefendable.

Steward: The official responsible for running the estate and feeding the household (from the word sty-ward who was the man responsible for the pigs).

Trebuchet: A siege engine with a large counterweight at one end of a long pivoted arm which when dropped swung the other end holding a projectile round, towards the target.

Wall walk: The path along the top of the walls behind the battlements.

Ward: A walled enclosure which usually refers to the open spaces within a stone castle (although these are sometimes still called baileys).

Wing wall: A wall running down the slope of a motte.

Beaumaris Castle: a militarily advanced medieval castle with concentric walls

Index

OTHER TITLES FROM COUNTRYSIDE BOOKS

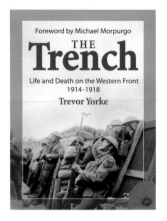

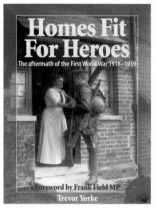

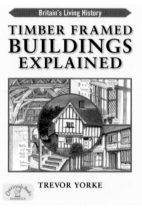

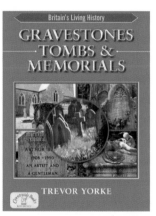

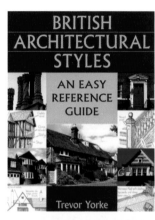

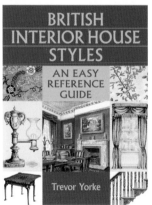

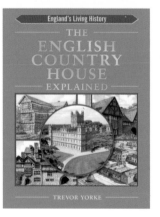

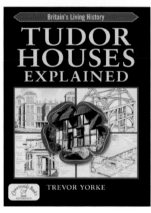

To see our full range of books please visit
www.countrysidebooks.co.uk

Follow us on @ CountrysideBooks